Growing Up in the OP

Tales of a Midwestern Baby Boomer

Richard W. Paradise

*This book is dedicated to
my departed parents, Barbara & Alfred,
my departed siblings, Mary Carol and Ron,
and my remaining siblings, Robert & Julie*

Copyright © 2021 Richard W. Paradise
All Rights Reserved
Editing by Dawn W. Petersen.
Cover design and formatting by Lori Bennett / loribennettdesign.com

No part of this book may be reproduced in any written, electronic, recording or photocopying form without written permission of the author.

Books may be purchased in quantity and/or special sales
by contacting the publisher at:
B-Say LLC
5416 West 97th Circle
Overland Park, KS 66207
rparadise@b-say.com

Printed in the USA

ISBN 978-0-578-82754-4

Introduction

Overland Park, Kansas, is a city of 190,000 residents, located in the northeast corner of the state, its eastern border but a few short miles from the city of Kansas City and the state of Missouri. It is the second largest city in the state of Kansas, with a land mass of 75 square miles. Its residents are comprised mostly of middle- and upper-middle class Caucasians, with levels of education and income that are above the national average. The cost of living, including property taxes, housing, food, and gasoline, are below the national average. It has a low crime rate, a high employment rate, an excellent educational system, and is relatively clean and infrastructurally sound.

Overland Park is similar to where many of you live and where many of you grew up. You will find many similarities to your own upbringing in the stories I tell, the places and times I describe, and the experiences I share. The quality and pace of life in Overland Park are similar to that of Dublin, Ohio; Crestwood, Missouri; Carmel, Indiana; Eden Prairie, Minnesota; Schaumburg, Illinois; or any number of midwestern bedroom communities that were borne from the labors of the Greatest Generation after World War II.

Overland Park is typical of the myriad American communities that within the short span of a generation went from dirt-road-cordoned pasture and hardwood forest to carefully plotted, densely populated subdivisions, interspersed with strip malls, schools, churches, and the occasional golf course.

Overland Park is where I grew up playing in new homes under construction. I had a fort in a drainage sewer that was built in anticipation and support of the spec-home subdivisions that would ultimately be built. I would stay out on summer evenings playing kick the can, dodgeball, or red rover long after the new streetlights had come on, but only up until my mother hollered me into the house for the third or fourth time.

Overland Park is where I grew up mowing lawns and shoveling driveways for my spending money, as such things as residential landscaping companies and snow shoveling services were virtually nonexistent when I was growing up. The notion of my father paying someone other than me to mow our lawn or shovel our driveway when I was a teenager would have been laughable, the stuff of science fiction.

Overland Park is where I had my first McDonald's hamburger, my first scoop of Baskin-Robbins Daiquiri Ice on a sugar cone, my first Black Cow at the A&W, my first slice of pizza, delivered to our home by the Villa Capri delivery boy, who actually lived next door to us and dated my sister.

Overland Park is where I got my haircut at Red's Barber Shop, where a chart on the wall had pictures of popular cuts from which to choose — The Flat Top, The Butch, and, my style of choice, The Princeton. My father would have taken me on a Saturday morning into this bastion of manliness, all but a ritualistic male rite of passing. Whenever the occasional woman would enter, the chatter and hum would come to an immediate halt, replaced by an uncomfortable but obvious and necessary silence.

Overland Park was where I went nose to nose with my first live lobster in a tank at The French Market. I jumped on my first trampoline at the Trampoline Park, sailed down my first (and last) giant slide with the aid of a burlap flying carpet, and played my first round of mini-golf at the Putt-Putt. I even rode on my first roller coaster at French Market Kiddie Land, which was but a red-headed stepchild to the primary Kiddie Land at 85th and Wornall, across the state line in Missouri.

Overland Park is where I learned how to ice skate, on the farm pond at the corner of 95th and Metcalf, which was once the main cattle pond at the New Dairy Farm, later referred to as the Manor Barn. The barn remained on the property, serving as a restaurant for many years and, ultimately, an appliance store, before making way for an apartment complex that inhabits the site today. Learning to ice skate on that Manor Barn pond came in handy when the King Louie Ice Chateau opened a short distance north of it, early in my teenage years. This was where I and seemingly every other kid in Overland Park would spend our Friday evenings, trying to make time with our eighth-grade female classmates — an unthinkable pursuit for me during the school day that I spent under the all but superhumanly watchful eyes of the Cure of Ars Grade School nuns.

Overland Park was where they built the grandest shopping mall that I would ever imagine, Metcalf South, until they built the next grandest shopping mall I could ever imagine, Oak Park, just three short miles to the west. I would watch Metcalf South being built, attend the ribbon cutting, hang out there on hot summer days, work there on cold winter evenings, and all but grow up, literally and figuratively, in its stores, restaurants, arcade, and theater. At that time, I never would have imagined that I'd live to see that beautiful, influential mall turned into a massive pile of rubble and eventually a vacant field, before my very eyes. I'd have more readily imagined witnessing the end of the world.

Overland Park is where I grew up. I may have left for a few years to attend college, and climb up the corporate ladder, and even chase a wild dream by owning a hotel in the mountains for a few years. But when you grow up in a place like Overland Park, Kansas, you really never leave, because Overland Park is far more than just a suburban city in a midwestern state; it's a state of mind, a way of life, a set of tenets that are ingrained into the way you think and how you put the rest of the world into perspective. It's a place that makes you realize that you are amongst the luckiest people on the planet to have this spot on the map as your moral and mental foundation. Overland Park, and the people who built it, gave you everything you needed not only to survive in this world, but to thrive. If you grew up in the OP, it was all out there for you.

Herein are my stories of growing up in Overland Park, Kansas They are no different than the experiences you would have had, and the stories that you would tell, if you grew up in Overland Park, or Dublin, Ohio; or Eden Prairie, Minnesota; and on and on and on. All of the stories are true. Many of the names of the people and the places have been changed, and many have not. I'll leave it to you to figure out whom might be whom, what might be what, and where might be where. I'll guarantee that you, or something you did, or someone you knew, or someplace you've been is contained in these stories. Perhaps this could even be your own biography.

The first three children of Barbara & Al Paradise, newly arrived in the OP, 1959

9154 Somerset Drive, our first house in the OP, on move-in day in 1959.

Growing Up on Somerset Drive
IN THE OP

My first recollection of being alive, i.e., one that I still have fleeting, visual memories of, was our moving day from Florissant, Missouri, to our new home in Overland Park, Kansas. This occurred in the spring of 1959, the actual date of which is unknown to me. My father had worked as a design engineer for Fisher Body, the division of General Motors that actually produced the car bodies, but was taking a big leap by quitting a solid job with an established, profitable organization to move to Kansas City and work with his three brothers-in-law in a start-up business. He took this risk with five mouths to feed.

I remember standing in our basement in Florissant, watching as my father took down the swinging hobby horse that he had built for my older sister and had attached to the overhead floor joists with rope. That is my first visual recollection of life. My second visual recollection happened shortly after the first, while riding in the back seat of our 1958 Chevrolet Bel Air, alone, my older brother and sister riding up ahead with my Uncle Chuck in his moving van. I remember following them and watching this big truck, loaded with all of our worldly possessions, including that wooden hobby horse, which would shortly swing in a basement 230 miles to the west, solidly rooted in the OP.

The Overland Park in which we found ourselves, while unrecognizable when compared to today's appearance, was solidly on its way to living out the dream of its creator, William Strang. When he founded the neighborhood in 1905, Strang envisioned a self-sustaining, well-planned, parklike community that had strong commerce, quality education, vibrant neighborhoods, convenient transportation, and accommodating recreational facilities — all amenities that today make Overland Park one of the best places in which to grow up and reside. His vision succeeded on a level that even the most optimistic of visionaries could never have imagined.

We were to ultimately end up at 9154 Somerset Drive, in a three-bedroom, two-and-one-half-bath split-level; actually, it would have been a tri-level, as you would walk down a short stairway to a family room/garage sort of arrangement, walking out of the family room onto a patio. This was the house where I can now close my eyes and visually recall memories of birthday parties, Thanksgiving dinners, Christmas mornings, and Fourth of Julys; lying on the floor of our family room watching TV and mooning over Connie Francis; peering around the corner of our living room into the kitchen long after dinner was over to see if my older brother was still sitting defiantly at the kitchen table, a plate in front of him containing only a pile of cold green beans that he refused to eat; a massive web in the front bushes housing what was possibly the world's largest garden spider; waiting at the front window for my parents to return from the hospital with my five-year-junior infant brother, as well as a thousand more memories.

It was from that house on Somerset that I was picked up by a school bus every weekday morning, along with two or three other neighbor kids who lived next door and across the street, and taken to Nall Hills Grade School. Here I would devote myself to the study of crayons, glue paste, and construction paper; and consume graham crackers and too-warm milk in the kindergarten classroom of Miss Pigget. That was her name; I am not making that up. I remember her as a curly haired blond with big blue eyes; I deemed her old, but she was probably in her early twenties. She was beautiful, and I now remember her looking like a slightly less sultry version of Marilyn Monroe. It was also on that school bus and in that classroom that I fell deeply in love for the first time. At the bottom of our street, in the large white house on the corner — the one with the big porch and pillars out front, and a swimming pool with a slide in the back — lived an absolute angel, with silky, curly blond hair and the most beautifully featured face that any five-year-old boy ever could have imagined. I never talked to her, but I used to imagine that we would be picked up by a double-decker bus, and the little angel and I would be the only two on the top level, where she would sit quietly as I simply drank in her beauty while gently stroking her golden locks. That implausible fantasy never turned into a reality; I never even knew her name.

My most vivid memory of our home on Somerset Drive was the black, wrought iron railing in front of the house that ran up the four steps of the walk to the front porch. I know my older siblings remembered that railing well, and I would bet that anyone from the neighborhood at that time would also remember that railing, for at the innocent, tender age of four years, I made that black, wrought-iron railing infamous.

It was a warm summer evening, and we'd just finished dinner. My siblings and I were out in the front yard, as were all of the other neighborhood kids, playing hide-and-seek, kick the can, or some such game that ultimately involved chasing each other around. That's what we did to occupy ourselves on warm summer evenings back then, and no one knew or thought any differently. I'm guessing it was a Tuesday night, because that was the one night a week that my mother got a break from her 24/7 job as a suburban housewife and mother to go meet with other suburban housewives and mothers and play bridge. I never liked these nights because my father was a lot less tender than my mother when it came to putting us to bed. I remember on one of those Tuesday evenings chasing my mother's car down the street as she headed off for her bridge game, screaming for her to stop and finally crumbling to the ground in a sobbing heap as her car disappeared around the corner, out of sight. More than likely, that visual was a lot more painful for my mother than her absence was for me.

This particular Tuesday evening I did not chase my mother's car, but was standing idly on the front porch, leaning against the black, wrought iron railing, when I heard my father call, "Richard, five minutes. I'm filling the bathtub." I continued watching as the older kids in the neighborhood ran around or rode bikes in the street. Most of these kids would have been contemporaries of my brother and sister, who were respectively three and six years older than I; at those tender ages, that sort of an age gap was profound. Without thinking about anything in particular, I took this remaining five-minute opportunity to see if my little four-year-old skull would fit into the space between the bars of that front porch railing. It took some effort, jiggling my head a little to the left and then a little to the right, to get my ears through the narrow opening. But I finally succeeded, wiggling my head fully through the space, my neck resting comfortably between the bars. I would have looked as if I were in some sort of a modern-day, suburban pillory, with my hands holding a bar on either side of my head, me gawking out at the older children whilst they ran free and unencumbered in the street. I called out to my sister at this point to see if she would notice my current situation; she did, laughing, and getting all of the other kids' attention so they could look and get a good laugh as well. The crowd of ten kids laughed, squealed, and screamed "Look at Richard!" They just as quickly stopped laughing, looked away, and got back to running around pell-mell into the waning hours of another warm summer evening. This all happened in possibly less than two minutes — it wasn't very notable to anyone, and wasn't what caused the incident to become famous.

Infamy was broached when, out of the eye of public scrutiny, I began to pull my head back through the opening. I quickly discovered that wriggling my head in an effort to get my ears through the bars was much easier than wriggling my head to extract myself from the bars. In fact, I was now finding it impossible to pull my ears back through the bars, and I realized that I might possibly be stuck there forever. I began to wail.

Just as quickly as my head through the railing had become uninteresting to the crowd in the street, my present plight and my associated howling had the gang of kids gathered around the porch, all delighted, pointing and laughing considerably more than they'd been laughing earlier. My sister Carol, six years my senior, quickly jumped to the forefront to see if she could help get me out of my predicament, but the more she grabbed and tugged and pushed and pulled, the more my ears felt like they were being detached from the side of my head with a burning lance, and the louder my anguished cries pierced the humid summer air. And, of course, with the amped-up anguish came more hilarity from the throng.

Finally, two adults entered the picture: my father and our next-door neighbor, Mrs. Boodles, she being a registered nurse. At last, I was saved ... or so I thought. I was to learn in my later years that Mrs. Boodles had a reputation as being somewhat of a lush, and on this particular summer evening, I'm told she was true to form in that regard. My father wasn't much of a drinker, usually limiting himself to one highball before dinner — I believe his poison of choice was scotch and water — so I don't think that alcohol had much of an effect on his lack of sound judgment on this particular evening ... but, I wonder.

After surveying the situation, my father tried to bend the bars open enough for me to pull my head back through. He was quick to learn that as easy as that might have looked, the iron offered too much resistance, and he would need some sort of mechanical means to open the bars. Unfortunately, he didn't have anything in his workshop at home that would force the bars apart, and he couldn't very well leave me there squalling much longer, the crowd now growing, the glee among the assembled swelling to a fever pitch.

Mrs. Boodles, she with experience as a labor and delivery nurse, looked down at me through slightly blurry eyes and began to smile, as if a light bulb had switched on in her gin-pickled brain.

"Lessh pull him through the other way!" she offered. "With that kid's big head and thosh big earsh, you're never gonna get hish head back through."

"That's true, Marge," agreed my father. "No question his head is bigger and wider than any other part of his body."

"Go get me shum hot, shoapy water," said the inebriated off-duty nurse. "I'll shtart getting hish clothes off."

And with that, Mrs. Boodles started unbuttoning my shirt, and off it came, and then my shorts, and off they came. None of this was done gently. My underwear stayed on, thank God, as the gaggle of neighborhood kids, and now a few more parents, all giggled with delight at the spectacle unfolding before them.

Out came my father with a silver mixing bowl that contained hot, soapy water, which he held for Mrs. Boodles, who began vigorously soaping down my upper torso, me wriggling and wailing to beat the band. This only brought on a larger reaction from the delighted audience.

"Hold shtill, will ya," barked Mrs. Boodles, "and keep yer arms at yer shide! All right, Al; think he's ready to pull."

At this, my father grabbed my head, tightly cupping his hands around my ears, while Mrs. Boodles went to the other side of the railing and grabbed me by the ankles, lifting my legs. It took but a second for me to slide through the opening, but much to my dismay, my tighty-whities didn't make it through the opening with me. What I thought was the ultimate indignity — having my head stuck in the railing — ended with what was truly the ultimate indignity: my small package of worldly goods being on display to every damn parent and kid on the block. I was released by my hysterically laughing adult supervisors (I said "adult" supervisors, not mature ones) to a robust chorus of laughter, cheers, and applause from the assembled throng. I awkwardly got to my feet, looking much like a newborn colt arriving into this world naked, wet, and slimy, its gangly legs kicking and searching for purchase on solid ground. I grabbed my underwear and rushed inside, my skinny little white ass the last vision of me available for neighborly chortles and guffaws.

I drive by that house every so often, and up until a few years ago, that same wrought iron railing stood guard over the front porch landing, its iron bars still symmetric and vertical. If only the current inhabitants knew of the sacrifice that was made by me, and my father, to keep them in such an orderly fashion.

However, in retrospect, I'm a little perplexed by my father's inability to rescue me from my wrought-iron prison without resorting to stripping me down and soaping me up. Alfred Joseph Paradise was an extremely clever guy, an absolute genius of a mechanical engineer. His job was to design machinery that manufactured and assembled automobile parts, which involved all sorts of moving pieces, i.e., pistons, valves, air pumps, limit switches, electric eyes, sensors, conveyor belts, and an assortment of mechanical things that were a lot more complicated than bending open malleable wrought iron bars, bars that needed to be moved but an inch or two, to free me from my embarrassing dilemma. Perhaps he viewed this as a teachable moment: Don't stick your head into a predicament without knowing how you're going to get out of it. Or, possibly, his pre-dinner highballs did have a hand in his temporary lack of mechanical acuity.

It would be extremely indulgent of me to get into the details of my family members in this book, as all of us have stories and particulars about our parents and siblings; mine are no different, and certainly no more interesting, than yours. But I also think it is important to lay the familial foundation for the stories that follow, and it is incumbent upon me, as a chronicler of the era and the locale, to give some background on my family. As with most of these stories, you should find commonalities in the people, the times, and the places; the mother and father, the sisters and the brothers. If you don't give a rip about reading about my mother and father, skip to the next chapters about the mall, adolescent sexual proclivities, and failed attempts at burning down portions of the OP.

Alfred Joseph Paradise, Jr. (AJP) was born in Hannibal, Missouri, in March of 1923, the second child of Alfred Joseph Paradise VIII and Margaret Ernst Paradise. He had an older sister, Joan, a younger brother, Paul, and two younger sisters, Mary and Judy. His father served in the Navy as a machinist on the USS *Canandaigua*, a minelayer that operated in the North Sea off the coast of Scotland during World War I, and came back to Hannibal to work for the Burlington Railroad, following in the footsteps of his father. I have fleeting memories of my grandfather Paradise, whom we called Granddaddy, as he died of coronary artery disease, and subsequent heart failure, in 1960 at the age of 63, when I was four years old. I got none of his good looks, or his expert carpentry skills, or his fine mind and quick wit; I did genetically inherit his inclination for high LDL and easily clogged arteries. Such is life ...

Being born in 1923, or thereabouts, consigned you to growing up during the greatest depression and most awful economic times the United States of America had ever seen and survived. With that experience came carte blanche to endlessly remind your progeny that every bit of food they put into their mouths, every bit of clothing they clad upon their bodies, and every shingle under which they slumbered, was something to be very thankful for, as they had none of this growing up during the depression. I say this slightly tongue in cheek, as anyone from my generation who was raised by depression-era parents knows and was daily subjected to this mantra. And any from my generation also know and understand how rough our parents had it and how damned lucky we were to have good food in our mouths; new, clean clothes on our backs; and a beautiful new house in the OP in which to reside.

AJP was eighteen years old, and soon to be nineteen, when the Imperial Japanese Navy Air Service bombed the United States navy base at Pearl Harbor, Hawaii, on December 7th, 1941. Two years later he joined the US Naval Air Force, and spent the war in Iowa City, Iowa, and Pensacola, Florida. Those two stateside locales played a major part in why I'm here and writing this memoir; however, AJP had two mishaps while stationed at the US Naval Air Station in Pensacola that challenged my eventuality rate as much as if he were storming Omaha Beach on D-Day. The pilot trainer of choice in 1943 was a beautiful yellow biplane, the Stearman PT-17 Kaydet, and AJP crashed one during a landing at an auxiliary Naval airfield north of Pensacola, in Foley, Alabama, and he ditched a second one into the Gulf of Mexico, just south of the Pensacola Naval Air Station runway. He walked away from one wreck, and swam away from the other. The US Navy was in no mood to give him a chance to dink or dunk a third plane, and consigned him to the engineering division, which allowed him to design planes but not fly and crash them. Good for him, and better for me.

The post-war GI Bill had him bouncing around colleges: Iowa State University, Cornell College, and finally General Motors Institute, located in Flint, Michigan, from which he graduated. He received a degree in mechanical engineering and straight away went to work for General Motors in the Fisher Body plant in St. Louis, Missouri, where he ultimately met my mother, who was a secretary at the plant. Oh, those were the days.

During his short stint at Iowa State, located in Ames, Iowa, he worked himself through school as a cook at a large-griddle hash house. Everything they cooked — breakfast, lunch, and dinner — was cooked on a large heated griddle roughly the size of your dining room table: eggs, hash browns, grilled cheese sandwiches, sirloin steaks, and hamburgers. Paper-thin steak burgers, with butter-grilled buns, fried onions, and a slice of cheese made a feast that would bring a tear to your eye today were it plated before you. Throw in some hash browns, and you're halfway to heaven.

Not unlike most of his generation, AJP was a tough father. We never doubted that he loved us, but showing love and tenderness wasn't his strong suit; that was my mother's role. Knowing his mother, my German/Irish grandmother, explained his lack of gentility, she as stern and cold as a bolt of winter lightening. During our school years, AJP would barge into our rooms at wake-up time and blast on the lights. "Wake up; rise and shine!" You then had a minute or two to rub the sleep from your eyes and gather your wits, because if you were still in bed after those few minutes, he'd come back in the room and pull down the blankets, leaving you exposed and shivering. If you lay there two more minutes, the final and always successful third chime on the AJP alarm clock was to grab and pull your big toe––toe yank, toe twist, and then blow out of the bedroom, leaving you bewildered, slightly traumatized, and damned wide awake. I'm certain he enjoyed this, but I'm not sure why. This nightmarish wake-up routine was a trait/flaw that neither I nor any of my siblings inherited and subjected our children to.

Growing up during the Great Depression generally seared an intense degree of frugalness into one's brain. Raising five kids on one salary also played a big part in promoting thriftiness and conservation. AJP pushed it to the limit. We weren't ever allowed to casually walk to the refrigerator between meals, open it, and grab a snack or pour a cold glass of milk. One gallon of milk split seven ways over the course of a week didn't allow for such unscheduled luxuries.

"Dad, I'm thirsty; can I have another glass of milk?"

"No, if you're thirsty, drink water!"

My cereals of choice — Corn Pops, Cocoa Krispies, Cap'n Crunch; i.e., crunchy, sweet stuff — were rarely purchased and, if so, strictly monitored, all but doled out with a half-cup measuring cup. I or any of my siblings could have polished off an entire box on any given morning.

"Dad, I'm still hungry; can I have some more cereal?"

"No, if you're still hungry, have another piece of toast, and drink the rest of the milk out of that cereal bowl! Don't waste it!"

"But I want some more cereal!"

"Too bad. People in hell want ice water!"

(We heard that one a lot from AJP. My guess is that warm bit of wisdom had been oft shared with him by his mother.)

AJP was way ahead of the curve when it came to recycling, but his concern for the environment was borne not from ecological concerns but financial motivations, collecting and cashing in on aluminum cans and soda bottles. Our daily newspapers were piled neatly in the garage and faithfully delivered every quarter to the newspaper recycling van that parked at our church. It was rare that a glass jar and lid got pitched into the trash, as most were cleaned and stored in the basement, where they would eventually be labeled and used for storing nuts, bolts, screws, and nails. Same for the empty metal Folgers coffee cans.

If you could build something rather than buying it, then that was what happened. AJP was an A-level carpenter, learning this skill from countless hours of helping his father in his basement workshop. He built a canoe out of wood slats and cloth, which he then slathered in a liquid fiberglass; he named it *"Gozinta,"* as in "it goes into the water." *Gozinta* was an awesome piece of craftsmanship, but it weighed a ton, and it was all we could do to get the canoe up the basement stairs. Were the neighbors alive today who helped pull off this feat, they would still mutter curses under their breath when reminded of their quietly unwilling participation. The rest of the civilized world bought luggage carriers for the tops of their station wagons at Sears & Roebuck, or Montgomery Ward; not AJP, who built a wooden and fiberglass monstrosity that clamped onto our luggage rack with wooden blocks and half-inch carriage bolts. It was painted it was painted white, splashed with bright, psychedelic flowers, was large enough to store all of our luggage and half of our furniture. There was never a problem finding our car in a zoo or amusement park parking lot. His handiwork morphed over time into sophisticated furniture, grandfather clocks, and beautifully constructed radio-controlled airplanes with six-plus foot wingspans — he never flew the planes, always worried that his creations would end up in a crumbled heap at the airfield in Shawnee Mission Park, not unlike his earlier attempts at piloting beautiful aircraft during WWII.

AJP was a "foodie" long before the term was ever bandied about. While he generally made us feel as if we were paupers, on weekends when he cooked, he fed us like kings. He was adventurous and innovative, making everything from scratch, and more often than not, without the aid of a recipe. He'd have something unusual in a restaurant and figure out how to duplicate it at home. Most Catholic kids had fish sticks for dinner on Friday night; we had battered and deep-fried smelt with hand-cut shoestring French fries. Every fall he'd drive down to a Mexican grocery store in the Argentine district in Kansas City, Kansas, and buy the fixings for homemade tamales — corn husks, masa, dried ancho and arbol chiles — and have friends over for the party of assembling the communal feast. He was an accomplished gardener, living every year for those first few bites of homegrown tomatoes, and sweet corn that had to be picked at the exact right moment, and eaten within hours after being harvested. In the front of our house we had a six-foot decorative gaslight that was landscaped with a variety of petunias; it wasn't long before those flowers were replaced with purple kale and kohlrabi plants, planted perfectly in rows that resembled beautiful landscaping but were in fact edible decorations. Whether it be gourmet six-course dinners for his couple friends, or the best hamburgers, fries, and chocolate malts in the city on Saturday nights, he never put anything on the table for anyone that wasn't perfect.

As stern and unemotional a façade as he tried to exhibit, at heart he was nothing more than a big kid, with a wicked sense of humor and a penchant for practical jokes. He loved fireworks and Christmas morning, building sandcastles and snowmen, going to the movies, planning and going on driving vacations, taking us fishing for sunfish and bluegill at Shawnee Mission Park on random summer evenings, and going to the Chiefs', A's, and then the Royals' games. On the surface, he tried to be one of those "all work and no play" kind of guys, but in reality, no one loved laughing and living as much as AJP. As hard as he worked to make us think we were poor, he gave us a life growing up in the OP that was simply rich in so many ways. Alfred Joseph Paradise, may he rest in the peace he and his contemporaries sacrificed to create for us.

Growing Up Catholic
IN THE OP – PART I

WARNING TO BOTH PAGANS AND DEVOUT CATHOLICS

This chapter deals with a variety of topics related to growing up in a Catholic household, being educated in a Catholic school, and attending mass in a Catholic church. If you are not a Catholic, or not familiar with specifics of the Catholic faith, there will be mention of practices and items that you may want to Google, as I've chosen not to go into the detail of describing the objects, or enlightening non-Catholic readers on the particulars of the rights, rituals, and dogma of the Catholic faith.

There are many devout, practicing Catholics who may find some of the material to be sacrilegious. My deceased parents, grandparents, and many of my aunts and uncles would petition to have me excommunicated for telling some of these stories, and to them, I apologize. For the record, I am a practicing Catholic; the level of my piety may be questioned by some, but I still actively embrace and practice my faith. One of the tenets I believe is that God bestowed upon us many gifts, amongst the most important of which would be a sense of humor, and the ability to laugh at ourselves and, on occasion, not take our convictions too seriously. In light and in spite of the following, hopefully He'll be smiling upon me, and with me, when we ultimately meet face to face.

Technically, Curé of Ars Church and Grade School, where I attended grades one through eight, from 1961 to 1970, isn't in the OP, but in Leawood, Kansas, two blocks north of the OP city limits. That fact has no bearing on the following stories, but I wanted to be accurate in the event that some of the locals who are reading this may be habitual nigglers.

Being educated in a Catholic school went hand in hand with going to Catholic weekly mass, which I didn't feel was such a bad thing, as it got you out of your class for ninety minutes every Friday morning. I also felt that it gave me twice as much cred with the Guy upstairs, when compared to my parents and most other Catholics who just went to mass once a week on Sunday. Shortly before 9:00 a.m. every Friday, the entire school would traipse through the halls in an orderly fashion, first graders first, sitting in the front of the church, and the eighth graders last, filling in the rows in the back of the church.

My early years of going to mass occurred before the changes in the service that the Second Vatican Council brought about in 1965, with the most noticeable difference to a fourth grader being that the mass was now recited in English, and not Latin. When the mass was said in Latin, and you were a second or third grader, it was nothing but a bunch of meaningless gibberish. Up at the altar, the priest would make some loud proclamation in Latin, and we'd have not a clue as to what he was proclaiming, but we were wired to proclaim back something in Latin, of which we had no clue as to what we were proclaiming, but it came as natural to us as putting on our shoes and socks. And all of this mumbo jumbo wasn't just spoken, it was sung, or chanted. We didn't give it a second thought, but I have to imagine that a genuine pagan, say like a Methodist or a Baptist, hearing this for the first time would think that they'd possibly stumbled upon some sort of creepy alien cult ritual:

The priest, proclaiming, "Domi Nos Vo Biscuuuummmmmm ... "

The second grader, proclaiming back, "Et Cum Spiri Tutuuuu Ohhhhhhhhhhh ..."

The nuns viewed mass with ultimate solemnity, and they certainly expected all of their charges to behave in the same manner, regardless of their age, or their inability to grasp why they were standing, then sitting, then kneeling, then standing, then kneeling, then sitting, all the while they were singing these meaningless singsongy chants. It was tough enough for a second grader to remain composed and maintain attention for an hour in a movie theater or at the zoo, let alone in mass, where you had not a clue as to what was happening, and you had the additional distraction of a bunch of your equally clueless, equally rambunctious peers to help you take your eye off the ball.

While the nuns *generally* viewed mass as a solemn occasion (they would have already attended 6:30 a.m. mass for fulfillment of their spiritual needs), during that Friday morning mass, the last thing on their minds was worship and reverence, as their prime occupation was continuously scanning the crowd for slipups amongst their charges. For example, if you were to whisper something to the kid sitting next to you, your nun would see it, always, and more often than not shoot out of her pew to come at you. Her oversized rosary, which was attached to her habit at the hip, usually along with an overstocked key chain, would go flying and clanking as she knocked over three or four of your innocent classmates to get to you and grab at the tip of your ear in an attempt to rip it from the side of your skull. If you were to dare try and defend yourself, she'd go full Moe Howard on you, pulling your hair out in tufts while slapping your face, leaving purple welts on your cheeks that would remind you for the next few days that talking during mass was something you did only if you were in the mood to sport purple face welts.

It was rare that a Friday morning mass didn't have three or four of these displays of World Wrestling Federation beatdowns. When we were young in the OP, before they had the WWF, they had *All-Star Wrestling*, which was broadcast live from Memorial Hall in downtown Kansas City, Kansas. I idolized Rufus R. Jones ("I got the hard head!"), Bulldog Bob Brown, and Bob "The Butcher" Geigel. I'm absolutely certain that the nuns never missed an episode, notepads in hand, as this is where they learned most of their torture techniques. The only difference was that *All-Star Wrestling* was fake; the nuns' brutality was as real as it got! I'm also betting that when *All-Star Wrestling* wasn't on TV, they were watching *Three Stooges* reruns for pointers.

I was the recipient of the ear-pull/side-of-the-head slap treatment three times during my stint at Curé of Ars. Nun beatdown number one was in first grade, when I was holding my nose during the part of the mass in which the priest burned incense to honor the host, or the Body of Christ, as it was displayed upon the altar in a monstrance. The Benediction happened at the end of a High Mass, which was a sort of amped-up version of a regular mass, held once a month. To this first grader, the scent of the incense was abominable, and without giving it much thought, I simply pinched my nostrils shut to avoid having to smell this awful, putrid smoke. Without my having the slightest clue what was coming — other than the unmistakable sound of swinging, clacking rosary beads — a nun appeared and slapped my tender little six-year-old hand away from my nose with her left hand, while simultaneously slapping the back of my head with her right hand. She did this so quickly and so deftly that if you'd been blinking, you would have seen nothing. From that day forward, I learned to tolerate the smell of church incense.

Nun beatdown number two came on one of the Friday morning masses when I was in third grade, during the quiet, middle part of the mass, known to Catholics as the liturgy of the Eucharist. I was kneeling, being good and minding my own business — not whispering or holding my nose — when I and all in the church were shaken from our prayerfulness by a loud, wailing "Oooooohhhhh ... ," which ended with a very loud **THUMP**, sounding something like the back of someone's head slamming onto the seat of the wooden pew. That is in fact what had happened, as one of my male classmates had fainted, making a loud "Oooooohhhhh ..." noise, and falling backward with full force against the pew. This happened in my pew, about three kids down from me, and it was quite a trauma for me and everyone else — everyone except the poor kid who had fainted, who was now out like a light, sprawled with his arms wide, much like the pose employed by the figure of Jesus as he hung nailed to the cross in the front of the church above the altar.

The nuns were quick to restore order, and in a short minute, the youngster was awake, sitting upright, looking bewildered and gingerly rubbing the back of his head. He was ushered out of the church, and things went back to normal, save for the fact that all of us were *FREAKED OUT* by what had happened, and thought about nothing even remotely religious for the rest of the mass. It turns out that the young man told the nuns he didn't eat breakfast, got dizzy, and the next thing he knew, he had a big lump on the back of his head with a nun standing over him in the pew. Naturally, he initially thought he'd done something wrong and the nun had coldcocked him with the spine of a hymnal, but he was informed otherwise.

Life went on for another month or two, and then it happened again. The church is quiet as the priest is up front at the altar, singing/muttering some Latin incantation, when the congregation is awakened from their reverential slumber by "Oooooohhhhh ...," ***THUMP!*** What the hell? Why is this kid skipping breakfast and scaring the crap out of all of us? After a couple of minutes he was back on earth, and back in class for the rest of the day as if nothing had happened.

The following Friday at mass, whom did I find myself sitting next to but Mr. Empty Stomach. I instantly asked him if he'd eaten breakfast, and he gave me a funny look but never answered, as he, and every other Catholic kid at Curé of Ars, knew better than to whisper in church. I was beside myself, worried to death he was going to scream and take the plunge while sitting next to me. So I did what any intelligent, thoughtful kid would do — whenever we were kneeling, which was when he had his episodes, I held both of my hands behind the center of his back, ready to catch him in the event that he deep-sixed himself.

Shortly into this, I heard someone behind me making the "psssssst" sound and turned to see Sister Mary Brutal making a really mean face at me and giving hand signals that any idiot would have immediately interpreted to mean, "Take your hands away from his back, turn around, and pay attention to the mass — NOW!" And then I did the unthinkable: I began to argue with her, in church! I mouthed something about my doing this in the event that he falls so I'll be able to catch him and save the congregation from the trauma of hearing his head thump on the pew. I then made a few hand signals of my own, which I believe Sister Mary Brutal unfortunately misinterpreted to mean, "You talking to me, Sister? You want a piece of me, Sister?"

She shot up from her kneeler, rosary beads and key chain clattering against the pew and a few surrounding students, her habit flying in the wind like an animated Rorschach blot, and leapt at me, all but demonic, *in church!* Faster than two blinks of an eye, she grabbed both of my wrists in her left paw and slammed them on the edge of the pew in front of me — where they should have been had I been in the required prayerful, kneeling position — and with her right hand, she smacked me a solid blow in the center of my back, all but knocking the wind out of me, and followed with an elbow rap to the top of my skull, it sounding to the congregation not much different than my classmate's head hitting the pew, which fortunately didn't happen on my watch that particular Friday.

My third in-church beating by nuns was by far the most spectacular, and certainly my most well deserved. I was in the fourth grade, nine years of age, and I'd just completed the training to be an altar boy (that's how we referred to it back then, as there were no altar girls when I was growing up). Being an altar boy, or serving mass, was something every young Catholic male had his eye on as soon as he started going to church. To me, the biggest reason for wanting to serve mass was finally being able to go into the heretofore off-limits back part of the church, known as the sacristy. This is where the priest and the altar boys dressed and prepared for the mass, where the vestments were hung, where the chalices were kept. As the Latin name implies, it was a sacred place, and when you were nine years old, it was pretty cool to be one of the few to be able to go into that sacred place.

I don't remember the particulars, but I believe we went to a couple of classes on the weekend where they showed us the ropes of serving the mass: how to light the candles, when to bring the priest the offertory items, when to ring the bells, etc. It was something you'd seen the older boys do hundreds of times, so you had most of it down by the time your turn came around. You'd officially be made an altar boy, and your name would immediately go on the list for serving mass, which would be a weeklong stint of either 6:30 a.m. and 8:15 a.m. weekday mass, or 7:00 a.m., 8:30

a.m., 10:45 a.m. or noon Sunday mass. But the big show was the Friday all-school mass, where you got to be in front of all of your classmates in general, and all of your female classmates in particular. Even at the tender age of nine, a man in a uniform drove the chicks crazy. (The uniform for an altar boy at Curé of Ars consisted of a black cassock, over which you wore a white blouse-type covering known as a surplice. When you slipped into this outfit, you felt sacred on a whole new level of holy.)

I'd been an altar boy for a couple of months, and had actually served mass maybe a dozen times. The thrill hadn't yet worn off for me, and most of my fourth-grade peers felt the same. You'd eagerly check the bulletin every week to see if and when you'd be summoned to serve. Your parents would eagerly check the bulletin every week to hope you weren't summoned to serve, especially the 6:30 a.m. weekday mass.

At a Friday mass several months into my stint as an altar boy, I was sitting about twelve rows back from the front of the church, on the far end of the center pews, adjacent to the side aisle on the right side of the church. In the pew directly in front of me sat a male classmate, another newly christened and anxious to serve altar boy. Directly across the side aisle from us, on the end of their five-person pews, sat two more fresh and eager altar boys. We were sitting quietly, waiting for mass to start. When the starting bell sounded, we all stood at attention, and ... what's this? There were only three altar boys serving mass, one short of the required number for the Friday morning all-school service. Someone didn't show, and now someone from the audience was going to need to get up there and fill in for the absent server. Very casually, as I was on the end of the row, I slowly stood and sauntered into the aisle, and began to walk up to offer my services. Also very casually, and simultaneously, the other three potential altar boys on the ends of their rows sauntered into the aisle and started heading slowly to the front of the church. So now there were four anxious, eager little mass servers who all had the same goal in mind, all oblivious to the fact that the math wasn't working.

The pace of us four quickened just a bit as we put two pews behind us. The light bulb went on in our heads at the same time, all of us now knowing that casual sauntering wasn't going to win us the prize; this was going to turn into a winner-take-all dash to the death. And then it was as if the starter's gun fired: server #3 in line took a lunge to get in front of server #2, but server #2 was quicker, darting ahead of server #1. Within the space of a few short steps, all four prospective servers broke into a dead run up the aisle. Just a few feet shy of the sacristy door, in an open area near the communion rails, server #2 horse-collared server #1 to the ground, with servers #3 and #4 tripping over servers #1 and #2, causing the scene to look like a four-child rugby scrum on the floor of the church, all trying to stop the other from getting into the sacristy door.

What I didn't get to see — and it would have been an entertaining sight to see, provided you didn't have any literal skin in the game — was the four or five nuns performing their own footrace and rugby scrum to get up to the front of the church to have first crack at this human pile of irreverent male malfeasance. I was server #2, the perpetrator of the horse collar on server #1, and I believe that act was behind me getting the brunt of the nuns' wrath. I remember my shirt being grabbed by nun hands on each shoulder, and being deadlifted in one swift, clean jerk up from the floor at a rate of speed that would have made Charles Atlas envious. I was then marched out of church, followed by three other nuns marching the three other delinquents, down that endlessly long aisle, in front of the entire student body of Curé of Ars — a walk of shame, indeed. With every other step, the nun would either slap me in the back of the head — *"How dare you disrespect ... "* — or yank on my ear — *" ... this sacred place ..."* — or elbow the center of my skull — *" ... to act like a Godless pagan hooligan ... "* — or punch me in the kidneys — *" ... during Friday morning mass!"* I thought that walk might never end, but I'm betting the nun wished it could have gone on forever.

On top of the physical pain I endured as punishment, I was barred from serving mass for the rest of the school year, which was way worse than the short-lived public pummeling administered by the nun. If memory serves, my parents weren't as upset about the suspension as was I, they being the drivers of the car at 6:15 on a cold winter morning when my 6:30-mass altar boy duty might have been called.

We all have phobias of one sort or another — some rational, some irrational. Many people have a fear of heights, and this would fall into the category of rational fears, as falling from a high elevation can kill you; the thing that those who have a fear of heights have a greater fear of is death. My mother was terrified of tornados, which is certainly in the rational fear category, while my father was rationally afraid of the destructive force of fire. Then there are phobias that fall into the irrational category, the likes of which are magnified as a child but quickly vanish when you reach an age of reasoning. As a kid, I was afraid to death of quicksand; it turned out not to be an issue as I got older. Another one for me, which came from watching the Johnny Weissmuller *Tarzan* films, was being captured by natives and having my legs tied to palm trees that had been bent and staked to the ground. When the natives whacked the ropes that freed the palm trees to swing back upright, you would be ripped in half. The thought of this gave me nightmares. It didn't ever turn out to be a real worry. And who could forget trolls under bridges? Absolutely terrifying. There were also guillotines and giant squids, these things seen in movies that kept me away from French haunted houses and out of Captain Nemo's *Nautilus*.

One last childhood irrational phobia that actually ended up having some teeth to it was my fear of local Kansas City late-night TV star Gregory Grave. He hosted the Saturday night *Shock Theatre* after the 10:00 news, coming on at the commercial breaks with kitschy, corny, bad-pun-laden comments about the film. There was nothing kitschy or corny about him to me; he gave me nightmares, and it was all I could do to watch him. As any good older brother or sister would do when they discover you have a weakness or fear, they find every opportunity to exploit it and hammer home the nail, pour salt in the wound, twist your sprained ankle, etc. Never in the history of the world have any siblings had a greater chance to inflict pain through teasing than what occurred between me and my siblings on a Sunday afternoon in May of 1962.

In 1962 we moved a mile south from our original Overland Park home, from 91st and Somerset to 99th and Briar, and who in the one-in-a-million chance would end up being our next-door neighbor on Briar but a gentleman named Harvey Brunswick, aka Mr. Gregory Grave. I vividly remember sitting in our Chevy station wagon, parked in the driveway of our brand new home, when my father got in the car after visiting with our new neighbor.

"Hey kids, you'll never guess who's going to live next door to us?"

"Who, who, who?" we all asked excitedly.

"*GREGORY GRAVE!*"

The two squeals of delighted laughter that burst out of my siblings' mouths were soundly squelched by my bloodcurdling scream and then honest-to-God tears. Fortunately, both parents stepped into the picture and tried to reason with their damaged-for-life six-year-old, explaining what a nice guy he was; he really wasn't scary, it was just makeup; etc. Turns out Mr. Brunswick was a prince of a guy, as nice and normal as his wife and the rest of his family. But he *was* Gregory Grave!

Childhood irrational phobias are eventually replaced by irrational phobias that are close at hand, easily realized, and can stay with you throughout the duration of your life. Let's take spiders as an example. It would be extremely rare for anyone to actually have their life threatened by a spider. Yet there are many who will recoil in mortal fear at the sight of even a small spider, no larger than a postage stamp. Giant, hairy, tropical tarantulas, while certainly more formidable, still are relatively harmless, not to mention the odds against stumbling upon one in your basement in the OP are immense on the side of the spider-hater. Yet, see one on TV, or say in a terrarium at the St. Louis Zoo, and you can actually be brought to your knees by a case of the willies.

I definitely have an issue with spiders, and I'm pretty certain it started with a large garden spider that occupied a big web in the bushes in front of our house on Somerset. As a five-year-old, I sat and watched this thing for days, transfixed, as it rested comfortably in the confines of its web a safe six feet away from me. While it was no threat to me, the look of it terrified me and helped send me down the road to arachnophobia. This spider fear would be compounded by a book in the school library, a large coffee-table volume of natural history that had a full-page, full-color picture of a giant, hairy, tropical tarantula, a picture that I innocently happened upon while casually leafing through the book during a second grade visit to the library. I almost crapped myself, reflexively throwing the book on the floor and, as you can guess, drawing a sharp rebuke from the civilian librarian. Thank God she wasn't a nun or I'd have had that book slammed onto the top of my skull while she was saying something like, "So, mister, you want to make noise by throwing books on the floor? I'll make some noise with this book!" — *WHAP! WHAP! WHAP!* — "How's that for noise, Mr. Funny Man?"

The fear of spider thing got bad enough that even when I was in high school I would call my father upstairs into my room to kill the occasional spider, knowing that he'd give me holy hell for being such a baby. But damned if I cared, because no matter what he did or said to me, it wasn't going to be as bad as having to deal with the spider. Tease me all you want, just kill that damn spider!

Twenty some years later, when I was in my late thirties, with children, we were camping down at Stockton Lake in south-central Missouri. We camped a lot back then, as it was affordable, and we enjoyed the outdoors, lakes, campfires, and all the other pleasures that come along with camping. It was in the fall, probably October, and as we were driving to our camping spot on one of the backcountry roads, a hundred yards ahead in the middle of the road, large enough for me to see even at that distance, was a real live tarantula. We were on it and past it quickly, as I was probably driving sixty mph, but I was certain that my eyes hadn't been playing tricks on me. Later that day, on a road near our campsite, as I was driving one of the kids to the bathroom, there was again, casually crossing the road, *another freaking tarantula!* I actually stopped the car close enough to watch the spider make its way from the road to the grass — rolling up my windows, of course — and Oh My God, I wasn't seeing things; it was a tarantula, in Missouri, less than one hundred miles from our house in Overland Park! When I got back home, I did some research and found out that there are in fact Missouri tarantulas, and they live in the southern part of the state, in wooded areas. For all I knew, the Missouri woods in which I'd been tramping and sleeping were crawling with these ghastly things. For real, we never went camping again.

Another of my irrational fears — and it is almost more profound than my fear of giant spiders — is my fear of vomit. Let's be honest, as I can't imagine there is anyone who actually likes vomit, but there are many amongst us who can deal with it when the occasion arises. It isn't just that I don't like vomit — I'm terrified of it. When my children were young and we'd be cruising down the highway at seventy mph, the slightest mention by one of my kids that they didn't feel well would have me risking the lives of my family and I, and God knows how many other innocent motorists, by cutting across three lanes of traffic in the space of about ten yards to get to the shoulder so my wife could get them out of the car before they puked. If you would have been watching me from above, it would have appeared that I was driving sideways.

Not only can I not handle other people vomiting, but I will do anything humanly possible to avoid me having to vomit. As of this writing, I haven't vomited since January 2, 2008. That's more than twelve years. But prior to that episode, I went twenty-three years without vomiting; I'm here to tell you, that takes some self-control. From where did this abnormal, irrational fear of vomiting come?

It was late one afternoon, maybe 3:00, and we were wrapping things up for the day in our second-grade classroom, where my teacher wasn't a nun but a very nice lady named Mrs. Dietz. I remember her as a pretty blond, certainly old (maybe thirty), but very calming and patient, especially after the holy terror of a nun that I had in first grade, whose job it was to violently burst the protective bubble of love in which we grew up at our homes, with our loving, caring parents.

On this particular day, Mrs. Dietz's relatively laid-back nature had us standing at our desks, talking quietly and just killing time before we would walk, row by row, to the coatroom to get our coats and lunch boxes before heading out at the 3:20 dismissal bell. There were five rows in the classroom, each containing six desks. As my name began with the letter P, and most often we were seated alphabetically, I was usually in the fourth row, and thusly, amongst the last to get to the coat room, the lunchroom, the playground, etc. (Such is the lot of a person whose last name begins with a P; better than poor Teresa Zipf, with whom I spent eight years at Curé of Ars.) As Mrs. Dietz called row one to go to the coat room, I happened to notice that one of the girls in the last row, she with a last name beginning with an S, was standing by her desk with a glazed look in her eyes, staring at nothing in particular but looking noticeably peculiar. I also noticed that her skin was the color of pewter, at which I thought, *Strange* …, and just like that, a stream of pewter-colored vomit projectile-launched from her mouth and splattered, with force, upon the top of her desk and the adjacent floor. It looked as if it had been shot from a fire hose. The image is still burned into my memory. Afterwards, she stood with her mouth open and her hands at her side, starting to teeter a little, looking as if she might just up and collapse into a heap on the soiled floor.

Dead silence from the class as all eyes turned towards a sound that is unmistakable even to a second grader: "Gag, gag, gag … reeeeeetch … splatter." My eyes were then drawn to a tall young boy whose last name began with an M, who started teetering as well, as his hand shot to his mouth, but not quickly enough to slow the cascade of puke that shot from deep within his gullet. Again, another vivid visual that is etched into my sixty-three years worth of memorable visuals. Then, a little girl in the first row, with a last name that started with a B, let loose a waterfall of the day's food and drink, this one close enough to the door of the room as to make us all inmates in this asylum of putridness. There was no stepping around it; you'd need to step through it to make an exit. We were all doomed!

Mrs. Dietz was panicked, calling on the intercom for the principle, Sister Mary Joseph, to quickly send the custodian, Mr. Sexton. "Sister, Sister, this is Mrs. Dietz. We need Mr. Sexton quickly; we've had several children get sick. Sister! Sister!" Poor Mr. Sexton was indeed the school custodian, a very quiet, gentle man who seemed to be ancient, but like all other adults to a second grader, probably wasn't much older than forty years of age. He always seemed tired, walking stooped over, and never very quickly. Come to find out a few years later, head custodian for Curé of Ars was his second job, as he had a farm in Oskaloosa, Kansas, where he no doubt worked like a dog all day, to then drive sixty miles and clean up after a bunch of little privileged suburban private-school kids, most of whom had probably only ever been to a farm on a field trip. And on this particular day, oh would poor Mr. Sexton ever earn his meager second income. He would need a fifty-five-gallon drum of that stuff custodians sprinkle on vomit, which actually makes the vomit smell tenfold worse than the normal heinous smell of vomit.

And then there was another liquid outburst from a child in the third row, followed by another from the left, and another from the right, then one from the front of the room and a final one from the back of the room — a literal quadraphonic symphony of retching and splattering. In all, eight of the thirty students lost their lunch in short order that afternoon; hard to believe, but I was not one of them. Possibly I was so stunned by this garish display of acid reflux that my body simply shut down, going into a state of shock. That's all I can think, as the smell of vomit was so overwhelming that it was an absolute, bona fide Catholic-school miracle that every kid in that classroom didn't hurl in place. You could smell vomit in that room for the rest of the year, or so it seemed to me. Without any further thought, even at the tender age of seven, I made the solid-gold life decision that not in hell would I ever be either a teacher or a school custodian, in the one in a million chance this scene would ever repeat itself and I may have some sort of hand or responsibility in the remedy.

Is the fear of vomit an irrational fear? I think not! Just ask Mr. Sexton.

At the core of a nun's daily reign of terror was her heartfelt desire to transform her students from slovenly, unappreciative pagan babies into educated, unquestionably committed Roman Catholics, with the ultimate goal being our individual quest for sainthood; nothing less was acceptable. In 1963, in Johnson County, Kansas, at Curé of Ars' Parish School, we were taught to believe that sainthood absolutely was attainable — it was all up to us.

I blew my chance at sainthood early on, in the spring of my second-grade year. I'd recently been blessed with God's Grace, having confessed my sins up to that point of my life to a priest in the Sacrament of Confession, and then having taken my First Holy Communion. To those of you who aren't Catholic and haven't experienced this physical and spiritual transformation, as seven-year-olds, we took this sacrament, this holy ritual, as being deadly serious, and for most Catholics, the seriousness of the ritual doesn't diminish with age. As a newly Catholicized seven-year-old, however, there was a bit more at stake with keeping up my end of the bargain with regards to being a good Catholic, as at that time I still had sainthood in my sights.

My second-grade fall from grace started with a lie — a big, spur-of-the-moment whopper; a lie that to this day I am still uncertain as to the source of its origin. It ended with the heretofore kind, reasoning, patient, and all-knowing Sister Mary Joseph, Principal of Curé of Ars' Parish School, kicking me square in the ass soccer-style (way ahead of her time!) with the force of an NFL kicker going for a sixty-five-yard field goal, jettisoning me out of her office and into the hall, me tumbling once, twice ... probably three times, head over heels. I knew at the end of the second tumble that my chance at sainthood was shot, and it's been downhill for me ever since.

It was a sunny spring day, lunchtime recess, the midday break consisting of twenty minutes to eat your lunch (which you ate in six minutes and fidgeted for the next fourteen) and forty minutes out on the playground. On this particular day, I was treated in my lunch to a box of Cracker Jacks, which, of course, in addition to caramel-coated popcorn and peanuts, came with "a prize in every box." My prize was a small plastic magnifying glass. The lens was maybe one-half inch in diameter, and the whole thing might have been one-and-a-half inches long; with my current old-man vision, I would need a bigger magnifying glass to even see this magnifying glass. Anyway, it was a prize, and I found myself absentmindedly standing in the warm spring sun, fooling around with it on the playground. Very possibly I was using it in an attempt to incinerate some ants.

Were this a film, you would see me in a long shot: a sweet, innocent blond-haired little guy standing on the playground, minding his own business. And then the soundtrack would begin playing something not unlike the theme from *Jaws*, as unbeknownst to me, the class bully was waddling his way towards me from behind. Totally unprovoked, the ogre whammed me in the back, his two chunky paws simultaneously colliding with my two shoulder blades, sending me face-first towards the pavement; in short, the fat bastard walked up behind me and without provocation pushed me to the ground. With cat-quick reflexes I shot my arms forward in time to prevent myself from landing face-first, but the downside result of this nanosecond reflexive act of facial self-preservation was the loss of the little magnifying glass, as it flew from my hands and was never to be seen again.

I didn't cry but was on the verge of crying. In fact, I was pissed off and quickly decided that this jackass had to have some payback. Unfortunately, none of the nuns or teachers on playground duty had witnessed this act of wanton aggression, and I didn't believe that much would happen to him if I ratted him out for simply pushing me to the ground. So I decided, as I walked towards one of the teachers, angry and wounded, to sweeten the pot a little. This pot-sweetening would require that I lie.

"Mrs. Daly, Claude pushed me and when I hit the ground, I lost my contact lenses!" I had no idea what contact lenses were, I just knew that they were small, expensive, and hard to find when lost. Not long before, my eight-grade sister had been prodding my father at the dinner table for contacts, and I distinctly remembered him saying, "No, they're way too expensive; we can't afford them. And they're very easy to lose, and very hard to find when you lose them!"

Mrs. Daly instantly sprang into action, blowing her whistle and herding all of the other kids away from the scene of the crime. She cleared out an area of about two hundred square feet, and instructed everyone to stand back.

"Where did you fall?" she asked, panicked, all but breathless.

"Uh ... right over there." I pointed to no spot in particular.

As if appearing out of thin air, there were six nuns on the spot, getting the lowdown from Mrs. Daly. Before my very eyes, and the eyes of the entire first through eighth grade recess crowd, the nuns got down on their hands and knees and slowly began crawling in the cordoned off area, their noses inches from the pavement as they scanned the ground. Like a rookery of arctic penguins searching the desert sands for ice cubes, they diligently pored over every inch of the playground, looking in vain for something that — like penguins and ice cubes in the desert — never existed. I didn't cuss as a seven-year-old, especially having just made my First Holy Communion, but I know the sight that lay before me caused me to mutter under my breath something very close to, "Holy Shit, what have I got going on here, and how am I going to get my ass out of it?" Even at that tender age, I knew that if you caused a nun to crawl around on the playground, in her habit on her hands and knees, because you might have lied, there would be unimaginably huge repercussions.

Enter Sister Mary Joseph, Principal of Curé of Ars'.

After getting the skinny from Mrs. Daly, Sister Mary Joseph went to the flock of nuns who were still searching in vain for the fictitious contact lenses and had them suspend their efforts. I watched in horror and fascination, along with the other three-hundred-plus students on the playground, as the nuns all slowly got up from their crawling positions and started dusting off the knees of their habits with their hands, their rosary beads and keychains clacking and jangling like a cavalry regiment of horses and their tack, with a few of the portlier nuns red-faced and huffing and puffing. Included in the crowd of those three-hundred-plus students were my older sister and brother, slack-jawed, both of them wondering just what in the hell was going on between this gaggle of nuns and their little brother. Sister Mary Joseph then addressed the gathered crowd, telling everyone to go back to recess, shooing them off with a wave of her hand. She then turned and headed over to me.

"Richard, I'm very sorry this has happened, but we don't seem to be able to find your lenses. Could there be a chance that you left them at your desk, or in the bathroom?"

"Uh, nope, I'm pretty sure I had 'em on when I came out here," I answered; another bald-faced lie, and to this high-level Servant of the Lord, no less.

"Well … maybe we should go inside and have a look, just to make sure. Don't you think?"

I followed Sister Mary Joseph into the empty school, down the hall and towards my classroom, knowing with every step that I was a dead kid walkin'.

Standing me before my desk, Sister asked, "How about your pencil box; can you look in there for me?"

I pulled out my cigar box, which held pencils, crayons, erasers — stuff that we used to write with before we had computers. I opened the lid and absentmindedly fished around among the contents, thinking, hoping, and praying that maybe I actually had contact lenses; *By golly, Sister! Here they are right here! How lucky was that?*

Instead, of course, I said, "No, Sister, I can't find them in here."

"Let's go look in the bathroom. Maybe you left them in the bathroom."

"Yeah … maybe I left them in there," I said, barely audibly as we headed down the hall to look one more place for my imaginary lenses.

Needless to say, I didn't locate the nonexistent lenses in the bathroom, but I did find that Sister Mary Joseph seemed to be getting a little suspicious, as her look had changed gradually from one of compassion to one of getting ready to call BS on someone.

Back up in the school office, Sister had me sit while she called home to give my mother the bad news.

"Mrs. Paradise, this is Sister Mary Joseph at Curé —

"No, no, your children are all fine. But we do have a small problem. It seems that Richard lost his, uh, contact lenses on the playground during recess and — "

My mother became *very* audible on the other end of the phone, and although not intelligible, I had a pretty good idea what she was saying.

"Oh really. Is that so? I see ... Yes, I'd be happy to let you talk to Richard." Sister turned to hand me the phone, and she wasn't smiling.

"Hullo?"

"What in the world are you doing? What in God's Name are you thinking? Contact lenses? What on earth are you talking about?"

She was yelling these questions at me pretty loudly. She had probably been leisurely ironing my father's handkerchiefs, thinking about what she was going to cook for dinner that evening, and then *this* call comes in!

"You know, Mom ... those contact lenses I had. I lost them when Claude Oafbutt pushed me for no reason ... *sniff* ... and I scraped my hands and knees ... *sniff* ... and it hurts really bad ... *sniff* ... ." I started to whimper a little, hoping the tears might buy me some sympathy, but my mother didn't have any sympathy for sale.

I handed the phone back to Sister, my head down, waiting for God knows what to come. I'd seen nuns draw and quarter kids for snickering in the bathroom line; I couldn't imagine the hell that awaited me from the Head Knucklebuster for this major misconduct. I assumed she got the top position because she could out-brutalize all of the other nuns, and I'd done some really bad stuff, stuff that would test her mettle and challenge her imagination as the head Minister of Punishment.

To my immediate surprise, all I got was a stern look and an outstretched arm, finger pointing down the hall as she hissed, "Back to your classroom ... Mister!" Just as I was walking out the door, starting to think, *Wow, that wasn't so bad,* Sister Mary Joseph made her attempt at putting her name in the NFL record books.

As I lay dazed at the other end of the hall, I recall hearing one of the other nuns in the office say something like, "Excellent form, Sister, and what a solid follow-through!" Coolly, Sister Mary Joseph acknowledged the compliment and said, "Sister Marie, please ... go get me the tape measure."

As I lay on the floor in a crumpled heap of personhood, I was too dazed to even cry. Not only was the blow first-rate, but the element of surprise that Sister Mary Joseph employed was a delightful extra touch, as I can remember, whilst I was flying through the air, asking myself *What in the hell just hit me?*, thinking maybe that Sister had a pet rhino that had gotten loose and butted me into oblivion.

I gingerly got up, dusted myself off, and walked back down the hall towards my classroom, feeling just a little sheepish. Thank God none of my classmates witnessed the launch, as it would have immortalized me and set my course as the butt of all jokes for the next six years of grade school.

Speaking of immortalized, Sister Mary Joseph is now immortalized in the *Official Record Book of Nun Brutality* for "Longest distance kicked with accompanied somersaults; male, less than 60 lbs. — 13 feet, 8 inches, 3 tumbles." And as far as my immortalization in *The Catholic Children's Book of Saints*, I don't have to tell you that not only did it not await me, there was never a chance in hell.

The year 1964 was a memorable year for me on several levels in that it was the year my sixty-four-year-old grandmother died, an unimaginable shock to me at the time, and also the year the Beatles hit the scene, an event that dominated our lives for the next few years. It was as if I'd been stone-deaf to that point in my life, and the first beautiful music my ears heard was "I Want to Hold Your Hand."

I was eight years old and in the third grade. I did not have a nun as my teacher that year, but a lay teacher named Miss Lange. I've no idea how old she was, as every adult seemed old to me at the time, but I would now guess her to have been in her early forties. She was not married, and she didn't seem to have a motherly bone in her body. I say this because some of the things I saw her do to eight-year-old third graders, and to me, were things no mother would do to a child, be it her own child or another's. I'm certain the nuns admired her sporting nature, probably thinking, "Sad she's a lay person; she'd make a good addition to the team ... "

There was a stretch of a week or two early in that third-grade year when I didn't own a belt, therefore, I would come to school beltless. One day Miss Lange called me out on this and told me I had better come to school tomorrow wearing a belt — or else; she didn't tell me what "or else" was. When I told her that I didn't own a belt, I believe she said something like, "Well you better go buy one then, hadn't you!" She said something along these lines to an eight-year-old! That evening I told my mother I needed a belt, with which she agreed, and she said we'd get one this weekend when we went shopping, and that was the end of that. I felt that excuse would suffice for Miss Lange, but on this point I was incorrect.

The next day I did indeed show up beltless, and the first thing out of the gate, Miss Lange spotted my sartorial omission. What she did next spoke volumes to the woman's perverse psychological makeup, and made one wonder *why* she wasn't a nun, as she certainly had the chops for the brutality side of the job. Miss Lange asked me to come to the front of the room where, before the entire class, she made me put through my empty belt loops a length of rope, frayed at both ends, which she had brought from home for the specific purpose of humiliating me. As we all know, no one can be crueler to children than other children, and the rest of the school day I was laughed at, pointed at, hollered at, and gawked at by every other kid in that school as I walked the halls looking like Elly May Clampett, she the most famous owner and wearer of a rope belt.

One small bit of vindication came from this awful incident. My mother called the principal, my old friend Sister Mary Joseph, and gave her an earful, telling her I didn't have a belt because she couldn't afford to buy me a belt until my father got paid the next Friday. I believe Sister Mary Joseph then gave an earful to Miss Lange, although, much to my regret, I doubt that she kicked her in the ass.

Things started to ramp up in third grade with regards to our curriculum. The math got tougher, with long division and multiplication. Third grade was the beginning of the SRA Reading Laboratory program, a color-coded system in which you advanced from rose to red to orange to brown to gold to lime to green to olive to aqua to silver, finishing with the stuff of first-place ribbons, blue. As you progressed through each color, the words got bigger, the sentences got longer, and the stories became more difficult to comprehend.

Third grade also had a few good things that we didn't get in second grade, one being the "art lady." This was a volunteer mother who would come in once every few weeks and bring a print of a famous painting. She would give each student a small copy of the painting, and we would paste it in our art books and write a description of the work. She would then discuss nuances of the paintings, the style, the colors, and tell us about the artist who'd painted the work. I recall one particular painting, a Japanese watercolor of people with umbrellas and rickshaws crossing a bridge during a rainstorm. In my art notebook, I titled the painting (having not been paying attention enough to hear and correctly write down the actual name of the painting) "People Crossing a Bridge in Jap." It seemed pretty straightforward to me, as my WWII-era, politically incorrect father referred to these people as Japs; I naturally assumed the country in which they lived was called Jap. (I believe we started studying world geography in the fourth grade).

Third grade also brought a more complex study of the English language and writing beyond the simple "My dog is nice" sentences of second grade. It was now time for more complex sentences and paragraphs. One of our major assignments of the year — not just an evening's homework, more like a term paper for eight-year-olds — was a multitasking event that involved mastering several skill sets: learning to use the library, learning to look something up in a book, reading, comprehending, and writing a report on what we'd read.

The assignment was to go to our public or school library, find a book of Aesop's fables, and pick one of the fables to read and write about. We were to briefly describe the characters and plot of the fable, discuss the "moral of the story," and tell how the moral related to our modern-day lives. That "modern-day lives" thing was a key element that I'd missed, as somehow during the lesson I failed to pick up on the fact that Aesop wrote these fables a long, long time ago, before there were phones, or cars, or orthodontists — all of which were present in the Aesop's fable that I would ultimately make up.

In what would be a recurring theme throughout my educational career, I procrastinated on this assignment to the point that it was due the next day, and I had yet to go to the library to look one of the fables up and read it. I did go to the *World Book Encyclopedia* that we had at home, and looked up good ole Aesop and read a little about some of his fables. I'd already heard a few of the fables in class, and I got the gist of them enough that I thought I could write a reasonably good fable on my own, with a protagonist, antagonist, problem, solution, and moral. Besides, I figured there was no way Miss Lange had knowledge of all of Aesop's fables as, according to the *World Book*, there were some six hundred of these stories, so this would be just another in the many that she'd yet to read and enjoy.

I have scant recollection of the fine details of my faux fable, but in general, it involved an orthodontist (my uncle was an orthodontist), and some sort of animal, and the conflict centered on who could fix teeth better, with the orthodontist showing the animal that *he* could fix teeth better. The moral had something to do with: Don't try and do things that you aren't very good at doing. Things like forging Aesop's fables. My story also featured twentieth-century accoutrements, such as cars, telephones, dental offices, and Bazooka bubble gum, that unknown to me at the time were not available as narrative trappings when Aesop was penning his classics. When I wrote it, I considered it nothing short of brilliant and believed that it would fit in seamlessly with the other six hundred fables that Mr. Aesop had written, and no one, including Miss Lange, would be the wiser.

The day came when the project was due, and up and down the aisles we went, one by one going up to the front of the class, reading our fables and dissecting the modern-day historical relevance of the moral lesson. When my turn came, I strode confidently to the front of the room, knowing that my fable would be unique — a refreshing break from the same old, same old that we'd heard from the first fifteen students.

As I stood before the class reading my fable, I'm certain that it took nothing less than a superhuman effort for Miss Lange not to burst out in uncontrollable laughter and call major BS on my literary canard. What Miss Lange *was* doing was looking at me in disbelief, with a half smile, half you've-got-to-be-kidding-me look on her face, which I took to mean that not only was she really enjoying this fable, but she was also pretty amazed that I had uncovered a new one that she'd never heard of. Hell, most everyone else in the class had either done "The Fox and the Grapes" or "The Hare and the Tortoise," and here I step up and pull this obscurity out of old Aesop's vault. She had to be flabbergasted!

After I completed my masterpiece, Miss Lange went off like a firecracker.

"Alright, young man! You made that up. Why would you make up a story when there are so many that you could have copied and written about?"

I immediately became indignant, fully intending to stand my ground and call BS on her, as I was certain there was no way she had all of the Aesop's fables memorized.

"I did not make it up! I found it in a book in the library!" I lied, now even convincing myself that I'd found it in the library.

"What was the name of the book, because it wasn't *Aesop's Fables*, because that was *not* one of Aesop's fables?"

More indignation from me. "It wasn't in the same book everybody else used; I found it in a different book. *Have you read all of Aesop's fables?*"

A bad idea to challenge her, as now she turned from incredulous to angry. But our argument continued. I laugh now at the thought of this forty-something teacher even taking the time to match wits with a seriously delusional eight-year-old pathological liar, but back and forth we went.

Miss Lange finally gave up and had me sit down, obviously exasperated at her failed attempt to get me to fess up with the truth, which, for the record, I never did. I stood my ground to the end, muttering under my breath as I took my seat, "No way she knows all of the fables. No way she can prove I made it up."

Fortunately, my shenanigans did not earn me another trip to Sister Mary Joseph's office, as even though it had been nearly a year since my past visit, my ass was still sporting the vestiges of nun-boot welts.

When my parents were informed of my little stunt, I again had to hear from both of them the old: "What have we done to deserve behavior like this from you?" and the requisite, "What on earth were you thinking?" And as much as I always seemed to have an answer to everything, the answer to these two questions, which would be posed to me numerous times throughout the course of my childhood, would never truly be known.

Barbara Jeanette Paradise, née Muehlebach, was born in 1920 in Kansas City, Missouri, and soon after moved to St. Louis, Missouri. She was the second child, and only daughter, of William D. Muehlebach and Willa Adamson Muehlebach. She had an older brother, Bill, and three younger brothers: Lawrence, Charles, and George. She was a doting sister, and they equally all adored her. It was very difficult for AJP to come into a family with four brothers who revered their only sister; from their point of view, no one was good enough for her, and damn sure not my father. I think in the end, AJP was accepted as worthy of my mother, but there were some rocky times along the way.

Prior to meeting, dating, and marrying my father, Barbara was a secretary at the Fisher Body Plant in St. Louis, Missouri, where her father worked as a purchasing agent. She didn't go to college, only secretarial school after high school. Barbara was from a generation in which many women felt that their purpose in life was to be a loving spouse and mother. She viewed it as her job, and she was exemplary in the performance of her duties.

Barbara was a wonderful, utilitarian cook, putting first-rate meals on the table every weekday evening, within the constraints of the tight budget, always served an hour after AJP came home, cleaned up, and unwound with his highball. She'd mastered the classics — meatloaf, beef stroganoff, pork chops and mashed potatoes — and still to this day it's hard finding a better plate of fried chicken than my mother prepared.

While my mom shared the kitchen with my father, she and she alone held the keys to the laundry room. Were "doing the laundry" a college major, Barbara Paradise would have been professor emeritus at your finest Ivy League school — a pity that isn't the case, as at least they'd come out of Penn or Harvard with something more practical than an elitist chip on their shoulders. Barbara sorted and washed everything expertly, never a shrunken pair of pants from an inadvertent dip into hot water, nor a red T-shirt pinking-up a load of white cotton underwear. She starched — always at the correct level of starchiness — and ironed every article of clothing: underwear, shirts, jeans, socks, and, yes, even AJP's handkerchiefs. She starched and ironed the things my dad carried in his pocket into which he blew his nose!

As far as cleaning the house, her performance was barely but a step below her world champion laundry prowess. A vivid childhood memory that stays with me involves my mother on her hands and knees scrubbing around the base and rim of the toilet of her three little males, coming as close as she came to cussing (which I never heard her actually do), saying tersely under her breath, "Why on *Earth* can't you *remember* to *lift* the seat and *watch* where you're *aiming* your *stream*!" A kid in my house could just forget about hiding contraband — matches, Playboy magazines, cigarettes, for example — in their drawers, not because Barbara Paradise was a snoop, but because she was so organized that when she wasn't vacuuming or waxing the floors, dusting the furniture, cleaning the baseboards, polishing the silver, ironing handkerchiefs, scrubbing toilets, or whipping up a meatloaf, she was organizing our dresser drawers. (Well, and maybe also snooping for contraband, a little.)

Barbara Paradise was also a saint, in the greatest sense of the word. She would never say, or let us say, a bad word about people. She was always positive and upbeat; she was never critical or sarcastic. And there was never a question that she deeply loved all five of her children equally and unconditionally. She'd say her favorite piece of the fried chicken was the back, not because she liked the back, but because she knew it was her family's least favorite part of the chicken and the last piece left after all of us had been served. She prayed the rosary every evening, more often than not as she waited and prayed for one of us to come home when it was past curfew on a Friday or Saturday night. It didn't matter what time you eventually did come home, there wasn't a chance in hell that my mother would turn out the light, lock the door, and head off to bed without knowing for certain that her children were safely in her home. You know what that meant — you had better watch and moderate what you were doing when you were out on the town, and you'd best be crisp when you came in that door, because you'd be talking and answering questions about your evening's festivities with the eternal sentinel.

Growing up with four brothers, Barbara was as passionate a sports fan as any person I know — Kansas City Chiefs, St. Louis Cardinals, Kansas City A's, and Royals baseball and KU basketball. She was educated and astute when watching the games, looking away from the TV only long enough to look down at her rosary as she reached for the next quintet of beads. In her later years, it became tough watching games with her, as she was a nervous wreck that all but ruined the game for those around her, loudly moaning and agonizing over every misplay. She'd never cuss, but would regularly belt out a "Catch the ball, you big dummy," or "Tackle him, you big dummy." Big Dummy was about as rank as it got for her from a profanity point of view.

Perhaps my mother's greatest strength, as was more than likely the case with most mothers of her generation, was her ability to coddle, shelter, and protect her children from the rough and tumble, emotionally devoid fathers of the Greatest Generation. I believe had us baby boomers not had these arbiters, these absolute velvet gloves blanketing the iron fists, many of us would have grown up a little rougher and a lot less sweet, and life in the OP would have been a much less wonderful existence. Rest in peace, my dear mother and saint, Barbara Paradise.

Almost Not Growing Up IN THE OP

Most of us routinely did things as children that, as we look back upon, would be considered all but suicidal: riding a bicycle downhill at breakneck speed with no hands, and certainly no helmet; climbing to the uppermost branches of a forty-foot tree, during a thunderstorm; shooting bottle rockets at one another, in the basement of a house under construction; tying a sled to the back of a moving car and hanging on for dear life — this one requiring the services of an older, but equally irresponsible, sixteen-year-old brother. When you consider some of the things that five- to ten-year-old boys did with their idle time when we were growing up, it is a miracle that there weren't weekly funeral processions up and down suburban streets with wailing parents and grief-stricken siblings. This also speaks to the resiliency of young, preadolescent bodies and bones, versus the bodies and bones of sixty-year-olds.

Speaking of sixty-year-olds, I'm old enough to remember when standing on the north side of 95th Street, and looking south down Nall Avenue, all you could see was a two-lane dirt road and empty grass fields and hedgerows. That would have been in 1959, the year in which my family moved to Overland Park. It wasn't long after that the developers started cashing in on the Greatest Generation's need for new homes for their growing families; in just a few short years, that same southern view from 95th and Nall was one of three- and four-bedroom homes with two-car garages, storm doors, chain-link fences, and cedar-shingled roofs. All of the streets in the subdivision that sprouted up between Roe and Nall from the east and west, and south to north from 99th Street to 95th Street, were named after trees that were planted in those suburbs by the various landscapers and developers of the area — cedar, linden, ash, rosewood, briar, juniper, and birch. What is mildly amazing is the fact that none of the streets were named after one of the most predominant trees that was truly indigenous to that tract of land, i.e., the bois d'arc tree, also known as the Osage orange tree, or the hedge apple tree. The area is still thick with these dense, gnarly, thorn-encrusted hardwood monsters. Planted who knows how many years ago as a natural barrier for livestock, the trees now separate neighbor from neighbor, depositing their utterly useless fruit — the hedge apple — all about the well-manicured lawns in the fall, and providing a sheltered utopia for the squirrels who make hay upon our bird feeders and our annual crops of tomatoes.

There was an old farm that sat on the land of what is now south of 99th Street, between Briar Street and Juniper Lane. An old farmer, his wife deceased, lived there amongst piles of rusted and decaying farm equipment, a small orchard of sickly trees that seemed to grow nothing but rotting apples, an old, unused barn with a stone foundation, and a small white house that I would guess dated back to before the Great Depression. The man had a garden that he tended, and he sold vegetables door-to-door to the few new houses on Briar, Cedar, and Linden Lanes — houses that were popping up like toadstools; houses that were unobtrusively threatening this man's livelihood, his property, and his very existence. Ironically, here for him now was a new, untapped market for his okra, tomatoes, and cucumbers, yet in very short order, these new customers would end up putting him out of business. I remember well the summer day in 1965, standing at the corner of 99th and Briar, and watching as the young developer's bulldozer flattened the old farmer's house and barn in a matter of minutes, and immediately after, the excavator came in to scoop up the vestiges of the poor man's life and deposit them in a dump truck. I wasn't yet introspective enough to understand what was really at play — here, on this day, at this time, and likewise throughout the history of humanity, one young man's rise is most often realized upon the back of an older man's fall.

From our small, three-bedroom, split-level house at 91st and Somerset Drive, we moved barely a mile south to 9943 Briar, into a house that had four bedrooms, plus an area in the attic that could easily be turned into a fifth bedroom, which my father did do in fairly short order. This all but down the street move was precipitated by the somewhat unexpected arrival of my Irish twins brother and sister. The first three of us came in manageable three-year lumps; my eldest sister was born in 1950, my brother in 1953, and I arrived in 1956. Looking back at this, it seems as if my parents, in a not so typically Catholic sort of way, had mapped the family out pretty well. By the time the next one came along, the predecessor was already walking, talking, out of diapers, and even old enough to marginally entertain themself whilst my mother was dealing with the newborn. All was calm and quiet on the family front until, BANG!, a fourth child arrives in 1961, and barely a year later, the fifth and final child arrived. It was during this fifth pregnancy that my parents assessed our living quarters and realized that the three-bedroom Somerset house wasn't going to cut it, and just slightly south we went, moving into the newly built Briar home in the summer of 1962.

The house had two stories, with a walk-out basement and a two-car garage. It had a large black walnut tree in the front yard, one of the few in the neighborhood that survived the developer's bulldozer. There was an eave that ran across the front two-thirds of the house, and a dormer window that rested on the roof above the garage. The dormer window was in the attic room that was quickly turned into a functional fifth bedroom. The garage was the site of my first stab at paid employment; actually, it was more like forced slave labor. For a weekly allowance of twenty-five cents, my job was to clean that garage every Saturday morning. You're thinking: *Wow! They forced a six-year-old to clean their garage — stack tires, scrub oil stains from the floor, set mice traps, and such?* Not quite. Cleaning the garage simply involved my father backing both cars out of the garage, and me taking a broom to the floor to sweep up whatever dirt, dust, leaves, paper, or trash may have accumulated over the past week. It was a simple task, easily learned and easily accomplished, although more often than not, I seem to recall that my efforts were usually judged by my father as being subpar. Unlike the game of golf, this was not a good subpar.

As cleaning the garage was not a particularly exciting task, there were a few occasions when my imagination got the best of me and I veered a little off course from the task at hand. The worst of these excursions involved my older brother, Ron — he, on numerous occasions in my young life, being the one behind the wheel on our veering off course from the task at hand adventures.

One exceptionally cold and rainy Saturday — so cold that the garage doors were kept closed — I was slowly sweeping out the garage, causing the dust to float and fog the air and my vision, when Ron entered the picture, I'm certain out of boredom. I remember that my mother, older sister, and younger siblings weren't home, just Ron, my father, and I. Most likely my father was in his workshop in the basement, or possibly in the aforementioned fifth-room addition, slaving away, and minding his own business, while assuming that I was competently taking care of mine. That assumption was, on this particular Saturday morning, incorrect.

Along the north wall of the garage, my father had a few fifty-pound bags of lime — calcium oxide, or quicklime — that he'd brought home from work to eventually add to our lawn. Calcium oxide works wonderfully for breaking down heavy clay soil, turning it, after a few seasonal applications, into the rich, black, arable dirt in which suburban broad-leaved fescue and Kentucky bluegrass thrive. Quick as quicklime, it'll make your emerald-green lawn the envy of the neighborhood. It is important to note that the lime product you would buy at a garden center is calcium carbonate, also known as limestone — simple, inert, nonreactive crushed rock — and it will also adequately serve as a clay buster. My father took advantage of his employment at a company that manufactured industrial adhesives, sealants, and coatings, and brought home calcium oxide, which is not inert, but very reactive. As to how it worked on the lawn in breaking up clay versus inert old calcium carbonate, it would be like comparing calcium carbonate to a can of Raid, which anyone can buy at any corner grocery store, while calcium oxide would be comparable to high-grade, highly lethal pesticide that requires training, a license, and professional certification to purchase and apply.

What does highly reactive calcium oxide do when it reacts with, oh, let's say something as simple and common as everyday tap water? A tablespoon of tap water stirred into a half cup of calcium oxide will react violently, shooting steam and hydrogen oxide gas into the air, while what was this seemingly innocuous white powder is now a bubbling cauldron of snow-white magma, its temperature rising to a point where the glass container is too hot to hold — maybe 130-140 degrees Fahrenheit. Safely handling the stuff should not be left to amateurs, and as any idiot could assume after reading my description of this material, never in hell should it get into the hands of children to be used for their entertainment. On that cold, rainy Saturday, the latter did in fact occur.

There were four fifty-pound bags of this slightly toxic powder stacked against the wall of the garage, patiently waiting for the warm spring day when they would be carefully poured into the Scotts fertilizer spreader and evenly distributed upon the verdant, yet agriculturally worthless, lawn that surrounded our house. Enter brother Ron. Whatever he'd been doing whilst I was sweeping the garage was now behind him, and he sauntered around the garage, saying something like, "Well, it looks pretty good in here. You've got it all about cleaned up ... except for *this*!" The calcium oxide bag on the top of the pile was open, and Ron grabbed a handful of the lime, compacted it in his hand, as — unlike talcum powder or baking flour — it compacted pretty well, and threw it straight above him, where the snowball-sized limestone smacked against the garage ceiling and, POOF!, exploded like a high-end firework and fell back to the floor much like the sparkled, spider-legged trails of a spent July 4th explosion. (A quick note to the reader: you might be thinking of Ron, *What a total asshole!* Not the case. Ron was an older brother, and anyone that has an older brother understands that's the sort of stuff older brothers do, especially on cold, rainy Saturdays when you're nine years of age and you're hard up for entertainment.)

Both of us instantly looked at each other with delight, gleeful to discover that whatever this stuff was, it looked really cool when you made it into a ball and launched it upwards to the garage ceiling. One after another, each of us taking turns, we'd fill our fist, and up against the ceiling it would go, and we'd stand back after each launch and watch the fireworks. I'm not sure for how long or how many throws we made, but before we knew it the air in the garage was so choked with the limestone dust that you could barely make out the naked ceiling lightbulbs. It was at about this time that we both simultaneously noted that our eyes were starting to burn, as were our nostrils and mouths. It was also about this time that we heard my father's voice booming through the murky air, as the door that opened into the kitchen, through which he was yelling, was obscured by the opaque atmosphere. Standing in the milky haze, we were totally directionless, the view was so clouded.

"WHAT IN THE HELL ARE YOU DOING?! WHAT THE HELL IS ALL THIS SMOKE? RONALD! RICHARD! WHAT'S HAPPENED OUT HERE!"

Neither one of us was particularly quick to offer up an explanation as to "what happened out here!"

Out into the garage came my father, accompanied by a series of coughs and "Oh my God's."

"What the hell have you been doing? Is this the lime? OH MY GOD! IS THIS THE LIME? WHAT HAVE YOU BEEN DOING?? DO YOU KNOW HOW DANGEROUS THIS STUFF IS?"

As intelligent as my father was, and as intelligent as most adults are — certainly relative to their young children — adults sometimes just can't seem to understand what would possess a child to do something that is ostensibly so stupid to an adult. It makes perfect sense to kids — an opportunity presents itself to try something new, something unique, and they try it, and it turns out to be totally cool, and while they're doing it, they're thinking: *This is so cool, I can't believe I never thought of it before, and now that I know about it, and know how absolutely awesome it is, I'm probably going to want to do it every day for the rest of my life.*

As unintelligent as my father was in being able to understand why his children would exhibit such stupid and reckless behavior, he did know the pitfalls of playing with a toxic substance, and he did not share our joie de vivre in our discovery that something laying fallow in the garage, when launched against the ceiling, turned into honest to God commercial fireworks. In a state of panic, he ran and jerked open both garage doors, hoping that the solid, dank outside air would help ameliorate the toxic choke of the fouled garage air. I can only imagine the view from the outside. If our across-the-street neighbor, Herman Rosenblatt, would see this white fog emanating from our open garage doors, at 11:00 a.m. on a cold, rainy Saturday, what would he think? What would anyone think? Smoke, but no fire? What Herman wouldn't see were the two young boys who were about to feel the heat of their father's fire.

We were both jerked into the kitchen and up to the sink, and the lack of tenderness in our father cleaning the quicklime from our faces did not go unnoticed. As the wet washcloth hit our skin, it felt like a rag soaked in boiling water, scalding our tender, young, prepubescent dermis as it wiped away the chalky acid from our faces, arms, and necks. What else was our father to do? He had to get the nasty stuff off of us, and the only way was to do it quickly, roughly, not unlike jerking a bandage from a mostly healed scab. Remember, there was not yet Google, where he might have typed 'gently removing calcium oxide from your mischievous child's skin.'

And then came the real punishment. After the cleanup, Ron and I were escorted back to the garage. The smoke had dissipated, and with the garage doors still open, the air was as clear as a bright winter day; in fact, the whole garage — floor, walls, ceiling, and every other object — looked as if it had just experienced every skier's dream of a gentle bath of a powdery snowfall. I was too young to understand exponentialism, but at this moment I was awakened to it: How could fifteen child-sized handfuls of upwardly launched limestone turn into powder everywhere, on everything — one-, two-, three-inches thick. It looked as if a dump truck full of quicklime had just exploded in that garage. We'd be sweeping the stuff up for months!

For a fact, it took us well into the late hours of the afternoon. A simple twenty-minute Saturday task turned into a daylong affair. But in the midst of it was a sibling bonding event that Ron and I lived and laughed with for the rest of our days. However, the quicklime party was not the near-fatal event for which the chapter is named, for several short months later, older brother Ron would once again lead me up a path that nearly led me to an untimely demise.

It was a sunny Sunday morning in late spring, and we were killing time before the family packed into the car and headed to Curé of Ars for 10:45 mass. I don't remember exactly what I was wearing, but it most likely would have been some nicely washed and pressed dress slacks, and probably some sort of expertly ironed short-sleeved cotton shirt. While only guessing at what my clothes were some fifty-five years after the fact, I know for certain that I was wearing leather-soled dress shoes. Slick, leather, shoe soles versus the rubber soles of sneakers were one of the key ingredients in the near-death experience that was about to unfold.

I'm guessing we had less than thirty minutes before we'd leave for mass, which was way too much time to just sit patiently and not do anything, but just enough time to walk a few houses down from ours and climb onto the roof of a house that was under construction.

We referred to new homes under construction as "work houses," because they were houses where men were always working. We were surrounded by them, block after block after block, as was previously mentioned this not-too-distant in the past farm and pastureland was under assault by the Greatest Generation and their booming families. They couldn't build the houses fast enough to satisfy the demand. And these homes were our playgrounds, their various rooms and closets, basements, ladders, roofs, and sandpiles making ideal locales for playing "war," which was essentially hide-and-seek, with the hidden being fake-shot with toy guns (or sticks, or even pointed fingers) upon discovery. Nowadays this sort of entertainment would be looked down upon, but to us it was just an ordinary extension of what our World War II-era fathers talked about, and it was also a good dose of what we were seeing on television with shows like *Combat!*, *The*

Rat Patrol, and *12 O'Clock High*, and in movie theaters with the likes of *The Great Escape* and *The Longest Day*. As children, it seemed to be a natural part of life to us, before we were old enough to understand the horrific implications of humans shooting at one another.

The work house of choice on that Sunday morning was three doors down from us, on the same side of the street. Actually, the floor plan was identical to our house, with the exceptions that the empty attic space my father converted into a usable bedroom was being constructed with rooms, and there were two dormer windows instead of one, which altered the roofline of the house, making it look ever-so-slightly different than our house. Our roof was one long, sloping line, while this house had two levels of roof, both shorter yet steeper than our house.

On that quiet, sunny spring morning before church, my brother Ron and I found ourselves at the uppermost point of the house, carefully teetering along the newly shingled cedar-shake roof. (Another boring, yet important, construction detail involves the difference between the surface of a cedar-shake shingle and a granulated-asphalt shingle. A new cedar shingle can be as slick as an icy sidewalk, whereas asphalt shingles have granules that make them all but slip resistant.) Ron safely traversed the peak of the roof, beckoning me to follow. I took two steps onto the sloped roof with my slick leather-soled dress shoes, and all but immediately, as would happen when stepping onto a sloped sheet of ice, my feet flew from under me, and the memory of what ensued lies eternally embedded in my psyche.

WHAM! — my body slammed onto the sloped shingles, my hands flailing to grab onto something. But there was nothing to grab. I slid down a few feet before I hit the three-foot drop-off onto the lower section of roof. WHAM! again, as my body landed full on its side on the lower level. The second impact actually slowed my fall a bit, but I vividly recall sliding down the roof and feeling the definition of every fat wooden shingle edge as my head and hips bumped against each, much like feeling every individual bump against your butt while sliding down carpeted steps. With every clack, clack, clack, my speed down the roof accelerated, and again I tried to grab at something to stop my fall. But as before, there was nothing to grab. In what was a matter of seconds, but seemed an eternity, I hit the end of the line and found myself free-falling the last, fast eight feet to the driveway. My body found purchase upon hard, clumped dirt, as the concrete surface for the driveway had yet to be poured. I landed headfirst, and the impact onto the solid dirt clods ripped a gash across the entirety of my forehead. I had no knowledge of this at the time. I remember slowly getting to my feet, taking one or two steps, and then it was lights out, as I blacked out and again fell face-first onto the ground.

One of the worst things about this whole ordeal was the piercing shrieks of the lady that lived across the street from this work house as she witnessed this whole event — from watching and worrying as two young children climbed across a rooftop, to my exaggerated slip, WHAM, roll, fall, WHAM, slide, and final plunge to the ground — the shrieking getting louder and more hysterical with every phase of my misadventure. She had been sitting in a folding chair in her driveway, probably tending to her own young children on a beautiful Sunday morning, and had to watch as this mother's worst nightmare — a live-action, slow-motion death scene — unfolded before her very eyes. I can still hear those screams.

Needless to say, I didn't die. I remember waking to the screams of the neighbor, and the ensuing wailing of the ambulance and my mother, as she ran hysterically down the street, *in her slip*, as her leisurely getting ready for church activities had instantly turned into fearing that she'd very possibly lost her middle child. An interesting aside that I later learned was that the neighbor from the street behind us ran immediately to the scene, picked my unconscious body from the ground, and carried me over to the street. His name was José Azcue, a Cuban-born baseball catcher who played for a short while with the Kansas City A's. That seemed to give my baseball-loving father some comfort at the time, and seemed to be one of his proudest details when retelling the story of my near-death.

The ambulance took me to St. Mary's Hospital, located down on Hospital Hill, near the Liberty Memorial, in Kansas City, Missouri. It's now hard to imagine St. Mary's being the closest hospital to 99th and Briar, as today you can't go anywhere in town without stubbing your toe on some sort of a medical facility. In fact, it wasn't then, as the closest hospital was Baptist Memorial, located at 66th and Rockhill in Kansas City, Missouri. I had been rushed there previously by my mother as a four-year-old, when they believed that I had swallowed the mercury-laden end of a broken thermometer, it snapping in half between my teeth as I was jumping on the bed, supposedly sick. I had been afraid I'd get in trouble for 1) breaking the thermometer, and 2) jumping on the bed when I was supposed to be sick, so I hid the two thermometer pieces under the bed and told my mother I'd swallowed it, feeling that would get me some much-needed sympathy as opposed to a much-needed scolding.

So, St. Mary's wasn't the closest hospital to 99th and Briar, but the closest *Catholic* hospital to 99th and Briar, and the doctor and my parents felt that my life was not enough in peril to risk having me be stitched up by the Baptists. The Catholics ended up putting about fifty-plus stitches in my skull and sending me home, so that I could live another day to climb another roof on another work house.

I pass that house on Briar now most mornings during my daily exercise routine, and as you would expect, I never fail to slow my pace a little, look at the house, and consider what could have been my fate. Unlike so many things that seemed large when you were little, and not so large as you got bigger, that roof is still pretty damn steep, and it isn't a fall that I would likely survive today. As I walk by these days and ponder the alternative to reality, I'm always cognizant and grateful that there was someone in addition to José Azcue that was looking out for me.

Ronald Alfred Paradise, the second child of Alfred and Barbara Paradise, was born in St. Louis, Missouri, in 1953. According to my older sister, Carol, she at the time sporting the wisdom of a three-year-old, Ron was puny, sickly, and colicky when he came home from the hospital, crying and wailing from the moment he came in the door. She said the same thing about me. Ron was three years my senior; he was my roommate until the age of ten, and my in-house teacher for all of the finer points of growing up. Most of the bad things I learned and the hare-brained, life-threatening things I did were either shared in with or shown to me by Ron. For a fact, that is the birth-sworn duty of any older brother.

Some of the kids I knew had big brothers that bullied them; that was never the case with Ron. The three-year gap in our ages contributed to that, as there was never any question as to whom was superior physically. We did the occasional "slugs-no slugs" thing when one of us passed, or pretended to pass, gas, but otherwise, our relationship was pretty nonviolent, which is mildly unusual amongst brothers. He was my coach, mentor, and teacher for all of life's arcanities, i.e., the important stuff that not only would a parent not teach you, but they absolutely wouldn't want you to know.

Ron was very smart, but he wasn't a good student. I remember my parents agonizing over this particular grade card, or that call from a teacher. We had to delay a vacation a few weeks because Ron, due to his less than stellar performance on the entrance exam, had to take a class that would allow him to ultimately attend Rockhurst High. Schooling aside, Ron was an absolute wealth of knowledge on all levels; he was as literate a person as you'd find, and had a memory for details that made me jealous. If you were in a mortal game of team trivia, with your life hanging in the balance, Ron Paradise would be the guy you'd want in your foxhole.

Ron got his start early in the ways of the dark side as a caddie at Meadowbrook Country Club, a private golf and swimming club located at 95th and Nall, which is technically on the border of Prairie Village and the OP, a short walk from our house. It was there, at the ripe old age of fourteen, that Ron learned to smoke, cuss, drink, gamble, and, most importantly, schmooze the older guys for whom he'd caddy. I remember him telling me stories of how he'd kick balls out of the rough for the old codgers, or run to pick up an eight-foot putt, calling it a "gimme." That was the sort of thing that got you an extra buck or two at the end of the round, and made that member request you by name from the overloaded pool of hungry, eager caddies.

Ron went from the golf course, to Rockhurst High School, to Kansas University, and on to a career of doing whatever he wanted to do that gave him joy. He married briefly, but had no children. He was a wine salesman and a nationally rated sommelier. I was dumbfounded by how much he knew about wine, way before it was fashionable to know about wine. He understood it from a scientific point of view, and used his indefatigable ability to remember quirks and details about things that related to vineyards, climates, grapes, and locales to make a living shaming a new generation of wine posers.

Ron lived a robust life, and his health from his self-embraced hedonism led to a struggle at the end of his days. On every birthday, he used to assemble and distribute amongst his friends a list of famous people that he had outlived — on his 54th birthday he was particularly proud that he outlived Jerry Garcia, an equally hedonistic guy he admired.

Ron was my hiding things from AJP muse, my prank phone call muse, my musical muse, my literary muse, my movie muse, my wine muse, and, most importantly, my getting the most out of life muse. He was the ultimate big brother; he was my first friend, my best man, and, throughout my life, he was my best friend. I was the only one with him when he died, and I believe that was the way that God intended it to happen. Rest in peace my dear brother, Ronald Alfred Paradise.

Growing Up as a Pyromaniac in the OP

From the dawn of civilization, the quest for fire has been innate in man. Not woman, just man. There isn't a male I know that doesn't like a good fire; and I'm speaking only of the bonfire variety, certainly not destructive fires. From my earliest days I have been fascinated by fire, almost to a state of passion — again, not on any level have I ever had any arsonist tendencies, but I also have never walked away from the opportunity to burn something in a safe and constructive manner.

The first recollection I have of actively playing with fire also coincides with my vivid memory of the only time my father ever put me over his knee and put a belt to my butt. I was six years old, and my older brother was a wise, street-savvy nine-year-old. He had come up with a "game" that he shared with me, a game that we would play four or five times over the course of the next week. The game involved a make-believe cave, matches, and candles.

For my father, growing up in Hannibal, Missouri, caves, Mark Twain, Tom Sawyer, and Huck Finn all played a large part in his childhood imagination and play routine. If you'll recall, Tom and Huck would explore the caves that riddled the limestone bluffs along the Mississippi River, upon the western bank of which Hannibal is situated, hiding from Injun Joe and figures of authority. My father and his friends got to know those caves as well. Today there still exists "Mark Twain Cave," a dimly lit, walk-thru tourist trap that Samuel Clemens may or may not have actually been in, but to us as six- and nine-year-old boys, it was the real McCoy. My brother and I were pretty certain during one of our visits that we heard the ghost of Injun Joe, moaning in eternal torment.

Taking a page or two from *The Adventures of Tom Sawyer*, my brother came up with a suburban substitute for a cave — the eave that ran across the length of the front of our house. If you don't know, an eave is the wedge-shaped protuberance that adds esthetic value, diverts rain flow away from foundations, or covers front porches. The eave on the front of our house was three-feet tall at the back end — the end that would be attached to the house — and an equidistant three-foot in length as it pointed towards the street, away from the house. On the surface of the eave were thick, heavy-grade wood-shake shingles, resting upon a layer of asphalt-impregnated roofing felt that was nailed to one-by-four wooden slats — a standard method of construction using typical materials. They still build them that way today, at least in areas where fire codes allow wooden shingles. The "floor" of the eave was half-inch plywood, affixed to the supporting two-by-six joists on eighteen-inch centers — that means one of these boards every eighteen inches, which we had to crawl over as we made our way to the back of the "cave."

To get to the mouth of the eave-cave, we climbed into the attic and wiggled around some boards and through some paper-faced insulation that my brother had ripped away from the wall studs, then got down on our hands and knees and slithered through an eighteen-inch square opening, and there we were, in Johnson County Cave. We would worm our way all the way to the back of the cave, some twenty-five feet, relying upon the occasional sliver of sunlight that would filter through a nail hole here and there to light our way. When we got to the end of the cave at the end of the arduous trek over two-by-sixes, while watching out for nails that protruded through the roof, the points of which would occasionally test the thickness of our tender, empty skulls, the real fun would begin; out would come the candles and the matches. We would sit huddled in the corner, in the darkness, and each light a candle, pretending we were Tom and Huck, hiding from Injun Joe. One neat trick we discovered was that we could use the flame to create soot and write our names or draw pictures on the wooden slats on the bottom of the roof — just like the prehistoric cavemen did!

So now you have the picture: two young boys, each with open flames, crammed into the far corner of a structure that was comprised of materials so flammable that just the hint of a spark would set them ablaze. If ten thousand different raw materials were made available to contestants in a bonfire-building contest, the ultimate winner would first grab the constituents of our cave in constructing the prize-winning conflagration. And here we sat, with those lighted candles and their flames less than an inch away from the wooden slats, writing our names in soot, the tar paper and the shake shingles, all of which the afternoon summer sun was beating down upon, raising the temperature of those materials to make them all the more susceptible to catching fire. If a fire had started, there was simply no way out for us; we would have without question burned to death in less than a minute. I am now certain that our continuance of this dangerous game would have ultimately had a bad ending — it was just a matter of time. Fortunately for all involved, divine providence played a part in our salvation from a violent, fiery demise, and that divine providence was candle wax.

Candle wax had dripped all over the legs of our jeans, evidence not only of our close proximity to fire, but also evidence of our blatant stupidity. I recall sneaking my wax-covered jeans down into the basement, where my mother reigned over her laundry kingdom, and putting them under a pile of clothes already on the basement floor, assuming that my mother would just scoop up the whole load and drop them into the washer, neatly washing away the evidence. There were two obvious miscalculations with this line of thinking: one, most everyone knows that candle wax isn't soluble in soapy water, and it would not be cleanly washed from the jeans, thusly, the evidence of our folly would be apparent to any who bothered to look at my pants; and two, not on any day, under any circumstance, would my mother cram a random pile of clothes into the washing machine without first segregating the colors, the fabrics, and the delicates, inspecting each article of clothing before placing it carefully into the washer. I've said it before and I'll say it again — if doing the laundry were a religion, my mother would have been in the running for Pope.

Shortly after I deposited my wax-stained pants under the pile of laundry, I heard a scream from the basement, coming from the lungs of my mother. I knew instantly where lay the source of her distress. Downstairs I went to face the inevitable, alone, as my partner in crime was nowhere to be found.

The inevitable involved my mother holding at arm's length a small pair of jeans, the legs of which were covered with a rainbow of colors worth of candle-wax drippings. "What on earth have you been doing? How did this happen? Have you been playing with matches? How am I going to get these clean?" The questions came in machine-gun staccato fashion.

As was my and most kids' modus operandi when confronted with a situation like this, generating a series of lies seemed to be the best way to initially deal with this issue, coupled with some grade A acting.

I stepped slowly towards the dangling britches, a look of absolute awe and amazement on my face. "Wow, will you look at that!" I said. "What is that? Is that wax? Are those my jeans? How did that get on my jeans?"

There isn't a mother of a six-year-old alive that doesn't know when her little angel is lying through his or her teeth, not to mention that the evidence of foul play was pretty compelling, plastered all over the front of my JC Penney jeans. It took a while, but she eventually got the story out of me, and, of course, I implicated my brother as the leader of this two-man gang of firebugs.

When the old man got home and found out what we'd been up to (my mother waited until after dinner to tell him, not wanting to ruin his dinner, while also making our dinner unbearable), the mood turned pretty glum around the Paradise house. While every adult is afraid of fire and its potential to devastate in a matter of minutes all that one has acquired in a lifetime — and that's if you're lucky it doesn't kill you in the process — my father was particularly afraid of fire, as he had experienced the destruction of his family home when he was a child (I believe he was four or five at the time). Even by the age of six I'd countless times heard his memories of him, his older sister, and his baby brother being grabbed up by their screaming mother and rushed from their burning home to stand in the street and watch the destruction, as his mother wailed in anguish, the neighbors making vain attempts to bring her comfort.

To this day I still don't believe he knew the severity of the situation, he thinking that we were just "playing in the attic," and not realizing that we were all but playing in a little wooden box, from which there was no hasty exit, that was heated by the sun and covered with tar paper and wooden shingles, writing our name on dry, wooden slats with soot from an open flame. I do believe my brother understood that we'd stepped across a line, a line that was way bigger than just "playing with matches," thus his insistence on not being specific about the exact location of our play.

Off came my father's belt, and first my brother, and then I, were draped over his knee, ass-end up, and strapped five or six good wallops with that belt. My father gave us the "this hurts me as much as it hurts you" line, and I'm pretty sure that he meant it, as he never was one for corporal punishment. And, believe me, there were many times before and after that we deserved it!

So what lesson did I learn from this once-in-a-lifetime whipping at the hands of my pyrophobic father? I learned not to play with matches in that particular highly flammable corner of the eave, from which there was no quick escape. I also learned that I needed to be more careful of the candle wax dripping on my clothes, as I now knew this would be a dead giveaway that I'd been playing with fire. And finally, I learned that if I was going to play with matches, I should play with them outside in the open air, or in grassy fields, or in tree houses, or in sewer pipes, or basements of houses under construction — or anywhere else other than that eave, for that matter.

For the next four years, I took a hiatus from my pyromaniacal tendencies, mostly due to the fact that my older brother had moved on to bigger and better things, and I didn't yet have the technical acumen necessary to pilfer matches and endanger the lives of my family on my own. Also, I didn't have playmates who shared my zeal for flame, as most of the kids I played with in that neighborhood were girls and, as we all know, girls just aren't that into fire. But that lack of a willing playmate changed when we moved into a new home.

In the summer of 1966 we moved just two blocks from our present house into a brand new one that my parents had built, sporting central air, a fancy tile-countered kitchen, a double oven, five bedrooms, three and a half bathrooms, and a variety of other bells and whistles that were making their way into the finer homes of the day in the late 1960s. Directly across the street from this new house resided my soul mate, my partner in crime, and possibly the only other kid on the planet that equally shared my passion for fires. His name was T-Gray.

T-Gray went to the local public school and was one year my senior. He was the fourth oldest of a family of six children, and his parents were a lot less restrictive than mine regarding what he did and where he was at what time. Summer evenings, T-Gray could wander the neighborhood into all hours of the morning, something that would have been unheard of in my house; I stayed the night at T-Gray's quite a bit the next few summers.

T-Gray wasn't much into sports, and there weren't enough kids around our age to spend time doing what most kids did, namely playing baseball or football all day. Our entertainment most days involved riding our bikes to the local mall, and every day visiting the small shopping center across the street from our subdivision, which contained the Kroger supermarket and a SupeRx Drugs.

When we weren't at the mall making life hell for the store employees, we were generally in some form or fashion looking for something to set on fire. We actually had a two-member club, the name of which was "Down with Smokey the Bear!" There was no purpose to the club — no dues, no formal meetings, no officers — it was nothing more than an attempt to define with a clever moniker what our life purpose was at that time. While the club had none of the formalities of other clubs, it did have a clubhouse — several of them, in fact. The main clubhouse was a three-story tree house in T-Gray's backyard, built by T-Gray's father. It was an absolute kick-ass structure with seven rungs up the side of a massive Osage orange tree to a large first-floor deck, which had a six-rung ladder that took you to a second-floor deck, smaller in size than the first; and finally, another six-rung ladder that led you to a third floor, or crow's nest, that was large enough for four normal-sized juvenile delinquents to sit upon and light small fires. Mr. Gray built this construction solidly and with a high degree of professionalism. He also built it with a strong eye towards safety, with solid rails surrounding each floor that were too close together for anyone to climb or fall through. As safe as it was, it was way high up, and I'm pretty certain that I never told my mother of its existence.

Our other club locations were "secret forts," most located in cleared, yet obscured areas of the tall, reedy weeds that were indigenous to the area, or in hidden, brushy areas within the stands of the many hedgerows, still prevalent in our developing piece of suburbia, known as Grasmere Acres. (I never knew what in the hell a "Grasmere" was, or why you'd name a subdivision with such a name. It turns out that Grasmere is an idyllic area in the British Isles — as verdant, pastoral, and peaceful a place as you'd ever find. Now I get it.)

These tall, reedy indigenous weeds that were the prevalent form of natural vegetation served a secondary, more important purpose than sheltering us and our nefarious activities. During late summer and throughout the fall, when these weeds would die, we would break them into cigarette-length sticks, clear out the white pith that lined their inner walls, making them into hollow tubes, and stuff them with finely crumbled, dead oak, maple, or hickory leaves, and smoke them like cigarettes. I remember them tasting absolutely horrific. I also remember one introspective moment, as both T-Gray and I were smoking/choking on one of these fire sticks, almost in a state of ritualistic reverence, T-Gray slightly holding the oak-leaf cigarette aloft in a pose of admiration, and simply saying, "Good smoke." I nodded my head solemnly in agreement.

※ ※ ※

Just west of our new subdivision, and separated from us by a dense hedgerow, was an undeveloped grassy field, approximately forty acres in size. Within but a year of our moving to our new homes, they would begin construction on a large, upscale, gated apartment complex, as well as a strip center that would contain a large grocery store, barber shop, clothing store, liquor store, etc.; the usual retail trappings of suburbia.

Three times in that same summer, we would set that empty, grassy, soon-to-be-developed field afire to the point where the local fire crews were called in to extinguish the blaze. It was never our intention to let the blaze get out of control, but the combination of bone-dry summer grass, OP July and August heat, and a steady ten-mile-per-hour wind made the conditions perfect for a pyro's dream, or a fire department's nightmare, depending upon your particular point of view.

Not only were we dim-witted and foolhardy, we were also ignorantly brazen, as during two of the three full-field blazes we stood all but enveloped within the heat of the action and watched, all but assisting, as the firefighters would douse the blaze, actually chatting back and forth with them and asking questions like, "What sort of kid would do something like this?" The third fire we watched from our window seat at The Drumstick Restaurant, casually dining on Toasted French Honey Rolls whilst slowly sipping our free ice water, no charge for refills.

Across the street from our field of fire sat the usual funding source for our tools of destruction, those tools simply being matches, or as we called them in "Down with Smokey the Bear Club" secret code: "M's." Riley's Gulf Service Station didn't have a lot going for it as a place where ten- and eleven-year-old boys would want to hang out, unlike the local shopping mall. But it did have, sitting in plain sight on the counter next to the cash register, an endless supply of Riley's Gulf book matches, intended as little promotional handouts for the car-driving, gas-buying, cigarette-smoking customers who frequented the gas station. I do not believe that Mr. Riley put them there to help fill the long summer days nor to fuel the desires of pyromaniacal fifth-graders; but in fact, that was the end purpose for the great majority of those little cardboard marketing pieces. And as I couldn't be caught dead carrying matches in my pocket, or bringing them into my house, we had a safe storage place for our M's — the empty battery compartment in the nonfunctional, softball-sized headlight on T-Gray's bike. (Nonfunctional? I think not. It was where we stockpiled our M's!)

Not only were the local fields an easy target for a conflagration, but shortly before my 1967 St. Louis Zoo vacation, T-Gray and I stumbled upon the stump and root system for a massive hedge tree — a tree that had been pulled out of the ground prior to the digging of a foundation for a new house. These hedge trees, known in the Midwest as Osage orange trees, were planted by farmers as fencing back before the invention of barbed wire, which, for the record, occurred near the end of the US Civil War. While the exact age of these particular hedge trees in our neighborhood was unknown, one can assume that they had been there for quite some time, as they had grown to heights in excess of forty feet; your typical Osage orange was known to be "horse high" after about ten years of age. Regardless of the exact age of the trees, all I can attest to is that they were damn big, damned stout, and they had a root system that, when lying on its side above ground, was easily ten feet tall. We climbed on them like jungle gyms, and made forts and hideouts in amongst the roots. One other fact about these trees and their newly exposed roots was that they burned, albeit very slowly.

The day before our weeklong trek to St. Louis and Chicago in the summer of 1967, T-Gray and I set one of these massive Osage orange root balls ablaze. It took some work, as the roots were still moist and green, but, by golly, we were up to the task. I remember driving down our street the next morning, heading out on vacation, and looking proudly upon the slowly smoldering stump of that tree. With more pride, I remember driving up our street, back from vacation after a full, one-week absence, and all but high-fiving myself as that tree stump, now reduced to a large pile of ashes and maybe a three-foot-diameter root ball, was still smoldering and smoking away. If only Mr. Riley knew what effect his advertising handouts were having on the local OP ecosystem.

Possibly the most stupid, most impossibly reckless thing I ever attempted involved fire, extreme ambient heat, wasps, and the house that my parents proudly built a few summers prior (and in which we were all still living; quite comfortably, I might add). This story should make solid believers out of those who are skeptical regarding the existence of an omnipotent higher being and/or guardian angels. What makes this act of insanity even more insane is the age at which this stunt was attempted. One would assume that by the time a person reached the age of twelve that he or she would possess, at the very least, an ounce of common sense. Yet based upon the sheer dimwittedness of this act, one would conclude that not only did I not possess one ounce of common sense, I may actually have had a negative amount of common sense, if that was possible.

This new home that my parents had built in 1966 was a large ranch style; however, unlike most single-story suburban ranch houses, it had a second-floor bedroom and bathroom that was visible from only the back of the house. This upstairs room and the accompanying large attic made for a very expansive roof. When you looked at the house from the front, the roof was by far its most prominent feature. At each end of the house, this large roof came to two dramatic peaks, reaching their respective apexes some twenty feet above the ground. One end of the house went toe-to-toe with the neighbor's house next door, which sat some twenty feet to the north. The other end of the house, and that impressive roof peak, overlooked our driveway and the street, as our house was situated on a corner lot. The driveway sloped down a little way towards the street, at which point that peak was now about twenty-five feet above street level.

This particular summer, the summer of 1969, was like all other summers in the OP — hotter than hell and drier than a Baptist's wedding reception, especially by the time August rolled around. By mid-August, the sun has relentlessly baked down upon the suburban landscape to the point where the bluegrass lawns are the color of bleached straw, and the streets and the sidewalks and the houses and the roofs are all sizzling and spent, they too as tired of the heat as the animate objects that trod upon them. Hiding from this pervasive solar assault by tucking themselves neatly under the slight protuberance of the wood-shingled roof at the apex of the majestic peak overlooking our driveway was a honeycombed wasp's nest, roughly the size of a cantaloupe. For those of you who aren't familiar with the physical makeup of a wasp's nest, that was one damn-big wasp's nest.

Next to big, tropical, hairy spiders, wasps are the members of the insect world that I fear most. (I've often thought that if there was such a thing as a big, tropical, hairy flying spider with a wasp stinger, which would hover slowly around you like a small drone, always threatening to sting or assault you, I would be left with no choice but to walk around eternally armed with a double-barreled shotgun. I've really thought about this, numerous times.) I think my biggest fear of wasps lies in the fact that in my sixty-plus years of living, with a lot of that time spent living outdoors, I've never been stung by a wasp, or even a bee. This has not been by happenstance, but is the result of extremely careful planning and my being painstakingly cautious.

Knowing this fact about me, you can now imagine that a huge wasp nest, attached to my home — albeit twenty-five feet above terra firma and posing absolutely no immediate threat to me or any others — was a constant cause of great disquiet to me. This was especially so at the time I was an unemployed twelve-year-old with a fertile imagination, an endless amount of spare time, and a brain that contained a negative amount of common sense. Come hell or high water, I was going to have that nest off of our property and out of my life.

There would be a few simple ways to accomplish this feat. The most effective method would involve spraying the nest with some brand of wasp-killing insecticide, more than a few of which were easily and commercially available. Possibly a high-pressure nozzle at the end of a water hose would knock those nasty wasps off of my roof and into another county? Nay ... impractical ideas both, as both would involve getting close enough to the nest to douse it with the poison or blast it with the water, and along with being terrified of spiders and wasps, I was really terrified of heights. And, of course, enlisting my father to eradicate the wasp's nest would have proved pointless, as he being a possessor of copious amounts of common sense simply would have said, "Nope! Leave 'em alone. They're not bothering anybody up there."

So there had to be another way of clearing my twenty-five-foot-radius comfort zone from those flying menaces, and using my lethal combination of a fertile imagination and the lack of a functioning brain, I was determined to find it. I happened to be farting around in the basement one hot August afternoon, when I stumbled upon my older brother's bow and arrow set. (Actually, "stumbled upon" is inaccurate, as my father had it hidden in the ceiling rafters for the specific purpose of making certain that he was around whenever my brother wanted to play Robin Hood.) This was a real bow that would shoot real arrows with real sharp, pointy, steel arrowheads that would seriously pierce and potentially kill a real-live person.

My plan didn't involve shooting the wasps individually with arrows, as even my internal idiot meter told me that would be a difficult accomplishment — not necessarily impossible, but certainly difficult. No, my plan involved fire, as I knew enough about wasps to know that they, like any other living entity, will not hold up well to intense, concentrated heat. Here was my plan. I was going to affix a ball of newspaper to the end of the arrow, leaving only the tip of the arrowhead exposed, set the paper aflame, and shoot it twenty-five feet into the air, right into the middle of that cantaloupe-sized wasp's nest. The tip of the arrow would pierce the nest, the nest would catch fire, the wasps would flee (many of them would even die!), and the offending nest would be no more. It was a beautiful plan on many levels: I'd get to shoot a bow and flaming arrow, which would be pretty cool; I'd be well out of harm's way in the event that I didn't get a direct hit the first time or two, which would end up pissing the wasps off; and, best of all, the key to this whole affair involved playing with fire.

I enlisted the help of my good friend T-Gray, as I estimated that I would need a person handy with a garden hose in the unlikely event that something went wrong with this plan and, say, for example, I was to set our house on fire. But I was pretty confident that I could pull this stunt off, leave the house standing, and banish the wasps through the Gates of Hades. T-Gray was less than confident; however, there he stood reluctantly beside me, bearing a charged water hose with a triggered spray nozzle, capable of shooting a stream of water some fifteen feet in the air — a full ten feet short of my intended target.

I vaguely recall T-Gray challenging me on the feasibility of this plan, asking if I was a good enough shot with the bow and arrow to hit that little target way up there, and questioning the possibility that I might actually miss my intended target and set the roof on fire. I also vaguely recall dismissing him with a confident wave of my hand, saying something like, "I'm a pretty good shot with one of these, although I haven't done it for a while." The truth was I never personally had shot the thing, I'd only watched as my brother recklessly peppered our backyard with poorly aimed, misguided, steel-tipped missiles. (There was a solid-gold reason why after but a few backyard sessions with the bow and arrow my father confiscated this weapon and had it stashed where he assumed neither my brother nor I would be able to find it.)

The first attempt was gratefully an absolute fiasco, with the flaming ball of paper dislodging itself from the arrow as soon as I let it fly from the bow, falling feebly to the concrete driveway, where it burned itself out in about five seconds. The second attempt had me wadding the paper tighter, so tight that it was almost difficult to pierce the paper ball with the arrowhead. When finally affixed to the arrow, fire was set to the exterior of the ball, steady aim was taken, and away flew the arrow, to smack harmlessly against the cladding on the side of the house, the shaft of the arrow hitting perpendicular to the wood-fiber siding a good ten feet below the target. I was starting to get frustrated, as what I had envisioned was going to happen was at that point the polar opposite of what was happening. I stopped for a second to gather my thoughts and survey the situation at hand, and as I stood there thinking that there was something obvious that I was missing that would be an easily identifiable root cause for my failed conquest of the wasps nest, a voice heralded me from behind, from across the street. It was our neighbor, Mr. Paris, a kindly, sixty-five-year-old retiree who, Thank God, happened to be watching this exercise from the safety of his home.

"What're you boys doing over there?" he asked. He asked this question as if he were dazed, and possibly in some sort of trance, as he couldn't possibly have believed that he was actually seeing what he thought he was seeing.

"Uh ... nuthin' Mr. Paris," I responded, standing in my driveway holding a bow and flaming arrow in one hand and a bottle of lighter fluid in the other, T-Gray holding a primed garden hose and some wadded-up newspaper.

"Well ... it sure looks like you're doing something to me. Does your mother know what you're doing out here?"

I wanted to respond, "Hell no, my mother doesn't know what I'm doing out here, because she isn't home, and there is no way I'd be doing this if she were home!" But instead I answered, "She knows that we've been trying to get that wasp's nest down (a bald-faced lie), but she isn't home right now."

Wise old Mr. Paris, who at that time was playing the part of God's referee in a game of Mortal Stupidity, rubbed his chin, and said, "Maybe you should wait until your parents are home before you try anything else. I wouldn't want you boys getting hurt. Don't you think that's a pretty good idea?"

Dejectedly I replied, "Uh ... yea ... that's probably a pretty good idea." T-Gray definitely thought it was a good idea, as he was chugging his head up and down in agreement.

So once again, providence came between my dim-witted, brain-controlled hands and a pack of matches, and disaster was averted. I know for a fact that Mr. Paris never told my parents what I'd been up to; I know this because I lived to tell this story, and, for certain, my father would have sent me away to a Siberian gulag at best, or beat me to death at worst, had he heard what I had attempted. At the very least, I'm certain that had he known of this idiocy, he would have had me sterilized to make certain that I had no opportunity to infect some other family's gene pool.

To say that I had a few close calls caused by my fascination and subsequent bad habit of playing with fire is indeed a bit of an understatement. In a fair world, my proclivities would have had me burned to death at an early age, thereby sparing the rest of my family, friends, neighbors, and all of the surrounding flora and fauna in our area the threat of their ultimate destruction at my hands. This isn't to say that I don't still have a few scars relating to my dangerous "hobby," such as the sixteen-inch scar running up my right leg and over my knee from molten plastic that dripped on my bare skin whilst I was playing with fire at a construction site. You should have heard the whopper I told my parents about that incident; I believe I told them I got it from pulling a toddler from a burning car, or some such other heroic act. It goes without saying that not only have I been fortunate beyond my lack of good judgment, but especially fortunate have been the innocents who've shared space with me, who bore me and raised me, and who continued to love me in spite of this little "character flaw."

All five Paradise siblings, shortly after moving into our second home on Briar Drive.

Brother Ron and I, sporting our new Christmas robes, 1961.

9943 Briar Drive, our second home in the OP. Just a whisker to the north was the residence of Gregory Grave!

Briar Drive house from which I fell in 1962. The circle marks the high spot summited, and from which I soon plummeted.

Our final OP family dwelling, it with the large, farmable corner lot and high, southern end roof peak, home to the almost-flaming wasp nest.

Al & Barbara Paradise, taken on their
25th Wedding Anniversary in May of 1974.

My brother Roberts 1st Birthday, March 25th, 1962, with the three older Paradise
siblings, and a couple of Muehlebach cousins thrown in for good measure.

AJP's homemade luggage carrier, which he painted to help stand out in the parking lots from all of the other homemade luggage carriers!

This is a picture of the actual radio controlled model Stearman PT-17 Kaydet built by AJP in 1980, which he never flew, nor crashed. It now hangs gloriously from the rafters of a beautiful party barn in Minnesota, a fitting tribute to the man who could build much better than he could fly.

A 1959 picture of the V-Shaped intersection of 91st Street & Somerset. The house still stands today, but the overturned cement truck, the object of my father's fascination, was quickly removed. Going through AJP's slides, I found no pictures of my First Holy Communion, or my Baptism, or my first day of school, however, I did find twenty or so pictures of this overturned truck, from every angle imaginable. Once an engineer, always an engineer.

A gang of local OP toughs, working the mean streets of Somerset Drive, Summer, 1960.

My 5th Birthday party, Summer, 1961.
View is looking north from Somerset, towards 91st Street.

The main fountain at Metcalf South, circa 1973. The Thom McAn Shoes store can be seen in the background, on the left. Dig those groovy threads!

The Glenwood Theater, in its heyday, amongst the finest of movie houses not only in the OP, but in the known universe. This fact isn't arguable.

Wonderland Arcade[1] and The Folly Burlesque. Not technically in the OP, but certainly a downtown Kansas City, MO magnet for OP youngsters.

[1] Missouri Valley Special Collections, Kansas City Public Library, Kansas City, Missouri.

Growing Up as a Delinquent IN THE OP

In spite of what you've already read in this book, I was a relatively good kid. I had some issues with minor delinquency, and I might have played a little fast and loose with the pyromania issue, but never did I engage in any hard-core delinquent activities. Hard-core delinquency would generally involve serious destruction of property or potential harm to people or animals. Shoplifting, bicycle theft, and breaking and entering would be pretty hard-core as well. I didn't do any hard-core stuff, nor did any of the kids with whom I hung around.

The foundation of hard-core delinquency, both then and now, was due mostly to the lack of a dominant male father figure to steer the moral ship. Everyone I knew and hung around with most definitely had that father, and all of those fathers were guys that grew up in the Great Depression, fought in World War II, and knew the value of both discipline and a buck. They all worked hard for what they'd acquired in terms of the basic material goods — houses, cars, nice front yards — and the thought of wantonly vandalizing these items would have never occurred to us as a thing to do for entertainment. In the event that peer pressure got the better of you, and you were to "farm a yard," or batter a mailbox with a baseball bat, you had better be ready to pay the piper if you got caught. The worry wasn't what the cops would do, it was what your dad would do to you — nothing as bad as the punishment nuns would mete out, but still pretty bad.

"Farming a yard" was a late-night activity that involved driving your car across the front of someone's lawn for the purpose of planting a destructive set of tire tracks across the surface of a beautifully landscaped expanse of emerald-green, weedless Kentucky bluegrass. Many of the yards in the newer, south Overland Park, upper-middle-class neighborhoods were often ostentatiously expansive; some of them as big as parking lots. And with that expanse came the owner's necessity to make it a showpiece — smooth, green, and manicured. A massive front yard not only screamed to the immediate world that one had the wherewithal to afford a large plot of land, but they also had the additional wherewithal to afford to let it lay fallow; the lawn just sat there preening, producing nothing but envy amongst one's neighbors. When a hard-core juvenile delinquent farmed a yard, it was often meant as an "Up yours!" to the status quo; a late-night, chicken-shit way to stick it to the man.

Our yard was on a corner lot, and it was expansive, much to my dismay, as I was the person responsible for cutting the damn thing on a weekly basis throughout the spring, summer, and fall. Also, with it being the corner lot, the lawn was a prime target for farming, as you could pull into the yard from the east/west street, drive full across it and off onto the north/south street. There was but one small tree at the time, so it was a wide-open expanse of unobstructed real estate. Our yard got farmed a lot, and I saw the ire that it raised in my father, he being the one that spent the time, effort, and money to keep it lush, green, and weed-free. It was precisely for this reason that the thought never occurred to me to bring this feeling of anger to some unknown, innocent person.

My father wasn't alone in his profound abhorrence of yard farmers, as most of our neighbors — they also being tough old cusses who helped beat back the Nazis and Japanese — shared this feeling of utter disdain. Measures were taken by many to put a stop to this practice, things like cementing metal posts into cinder blocks, painting them black for nighttime camouflage, and strategically placing them in the expanse of bluegrass. You smack into one of these land mines and you're going to need to make a trip to the insurance adjuster. Another clever detriment was to hammer six-inch, ten-penny nails through twelve-foot-long, one-by-four boards, so that the nails stuck menacingly through the board, and place these boards, with the nails exposed, surreptitiously throughout the thoroughfare part of the lawn, giving the unsuspecting farmer two flat tires in short order if he was unlucky enough to drive over them. This, in fact, happened to some young punk while farming a yard in the subdivision of Apple Valley, which was full of houses that possessed some pretty spectacular expanses of grass. The homeowner, who'd been lying in wait for such an event, pulled the kid out of the disabled vehicle and beat the crap out of him, while a few of the man's neighbors cheered him on. You do that nowadays and at best you're looking at a lawsuit, and more likely an assault charge to go along with it. Back then, they all figured the little hoodlum had it coming to him. I'm telling you, these guys hated having their yards farmed!

In the seventh grade, we had a new kid move to Overland Park from the other side of the world (I believe he lived previously in Tulsa), and as he was kind of smallish and scruffy looking, my immediate group of equally small and scruffy-looking friends befriended him. He was a bit of a smart-ass, sassing the nuns once or twice before he learned that got him a poke in the eye with a wooden pointer, or his face smashed and held onto the surface of his desk for a long minute. Where he really separated himself from me and my non hard-core friends was on Halloween, the night that brought out a little bit of devil in the best of kids and, on this particular night, the night that allowed this reprobate from Tulsa to all but foam at the mouth thinking about the one night in the year that minor mischief is expected, and mildly tolerated.

We began working the nice neighborhoods north of 95th Street and west of Mission Road (technically, in Prairie Village, Kansas), where the word on the street was "full-sized candy bars, baby!" — none of these mini Three Musketeers or Butterfingers, or, God forbid, apples, orange foam candy peanuts, or peppermint lozenges similar to what you'd fill your pockets with after eating at Putsch's Cafeteria. Right out of the gate, the first house we went to, after getting our candy from some nice lady that reminded me a lot of my mother — and everyone else's mother for that matter — no sooner had the door shut than this Okie psycho picks up the carved pumpkin, lifts it above his head, and smashes it solidly on the very porch where the nice lady had just blessed us with kind words and free candy. While I never smashed a pumpkin, the general rule of acceptability for pumpkin smashing was that you did it at the end of the evening, and you did it in the street, not on the porch.

The next house we visited had a small walled courtyard with a fountain in the center. The fountain was about four feet high, a sort of birdbath on a pedestal arrangement, with an armed Venus de Milo-type statue (not armed with guns, but armed with arms) holding a vase that spewed water into the birdbath pool. This was pretty high-rent stuff to me, and I remember commenting to myself how awesome it would be to have this sort of decoration in your front entryway. This extravagance wasn't lost on my trick-or-treating friend from Tulsa, as he commented with a touch of drama, Eddie Haskell-style, to the nice woman that lived at the house and gave us our candy.

"Ma'am, that sure is a beautiful fountain you have. And thank you very much for the candy. Have a very Happy Halloween!"

"Why, thank you very much," she responded. "You boys have fun tonight, and be careful!"

With that, our benefactor quietly closed the door and headed back to whatever she was watching on TV, absentmindedly waiting for the next "ding-dong" that would bring sugar-starved hobgoblins to her wonderful entryway. We headed out of the courtyard, all except for one, our friend from Tulsa, who Bruce Lee-ed the birdbath part of the fountain with a left foot kick, and toppled the whole decorative concrete arrangement to the floor, the force of landing causing the armed Venus de Milo to indeed become a suitable armless replica of the famous Louvre resident. The hoodlum cackled in delight, while the rest of the party was disgraced and somber.

A couple of houses later, we tricked-or-treated a large ranch home, which in addition to the main door, had a large sliding door with a sliding screen that was located on the front of the house between the main door and the garage. Ding-dong! Another lady much like my mother opens the door and offers us a large bowl filled with the mini Snickers, Baby Ruths, and Milky Ways. "Help yourselves, boys. My, aren't you all scary looking. Be careful tonight!" This was followed by a chorus of thank-yous as we stepped off the porch and headed down the walk towards the next house. All of us except for our new friend from Tulsa, that is, who stopped at the screened sliding door, sized it up for a few seconds, and then pulled a fairly large folding knife from his jacket pocket and slashed the screen door diagonally from stem to stern as deftly as if he'd been doing it for a living.

Not only had I never seen anything like it, I'd never imagined anything like it. I didn't use the term "WTF!" back then, but that would have been a good night to adopt it into my vocabulary, because that's about what I thought. That may be how they roll in Oklahoma, but we didn't roll that way in the OP. My immediate best friend in the group and I slowed our walk until we distanced ourselves from the rest, and after waiting a few more minutes, we headed off in another direction and left Mr. Fountain-Wrecking-Screen-Slasher for the night. I wanted none of this, as I figured he was just getting warmed up, and I imagined the night wasn't going to end well for him and the rest of the crew that was goading him on. I wasn't an angel, but I damn sure wasn't wired for hard-core.

✳ ✳ ✳

The entertainment options for kids today are all but infinite due to technology. A kid can — and many kids do — entertain themselves every waking hour with the internet, video games, Netflix, ten thousand cable channels, and smart phones. Many in my generation wring their hands over this, thinking the younger generations are wasting their lives away by not being outside doing the sorts of things that we did when we didn't have technology. You can also look at it another way. Had we technology to keep us busy, we might not have spent all of our idle time outdoors using our imaginations to find ways to get into mischief. For when all you had was a black-and-white with three channels to entertain you, you'd better have had an imagination and some wide-open spaces or it would make for a painfully long summer.

Wait a minute. We did have a piece of technology that we occasionally played with — the telephone. Other than occasionally building and burning a good fire, there wasn't much we enjoyed doing more than making prank phone calls. Caller ID has pretty much killed that entertaining pastime, and it's a damn shame, because nothing could create more unbridled mirth than suckering some stranger into opening their refrigerator door to see if it was running.

We had two phones in our house: one in the kitchen and one in the upstairs hallway. As soon as our parents' car exhaust fumes were the only sign left of them, I'd run upstairs to man the hallway phone, while brother Ron would handle the dialing duties in the kitchen. He'd go to a random page in the phone book, pick a random number, dial, and while the phone was ringing, he'd yell up at me, "PICK IT UP! IT'S RINGING," which was my cue to lift the receiver and listen in. I'd cover the mouthpiece with my hand, because nothing would tip off an unsuspecting dupe quicker than a nine-year-old's giggle mixed in with the faux official-sounding voice of a twelve-year-old.

"Hello."

"Yes, is this Mrs. Effbaum?"

"Yes, it is."

"Mrs. Effbaum, my name is Ben Dover, and I'm with Kansas City Power & Light, and we're doing a survey. Could you tell me if your refrigerator is running?"

"Sure, just a minute." (Ten-second pause, some muffled noises coming from the background.) "Why yes ... yes it is!"

"Well, don't you think you'd better run and catch it!" Hang up, and let the unbridled mirth come raining down.

Another one of Ron's classic routines involved calling the same person repeatedly, with maybe a ten-minute break between calls.

"Hello."

"Yes, may I speak with Ramone?" (He'd use some sort of a bad Latino accent, and vary it a little with every call.)

"I'm sorry, you must have the wrong number."

"This isn't Ramone's number?"

"No, I'm sorry, you have the wrong number."

"Well, can you do me a favor and tell him that José called?"

He'd then immediately hang up.

After about five of these calls, each one using a different name for the message to be given to Ramone (Juan, Paco, Jesus, etc.), the party on the other line would start getting a little short-tempered. Finally, on the sixth call, without even waiting for my brother to speak:

"WHO IS THIS? WHY DO YOU KEEP CALLING ME?"

"Oh, hi. This is Ramone, and I'm just calling to see if I have any messages."

Again, unbridled mirth.

There were numerous other pranks and gags, such as ordering pizzas for delivery to strangers, or making appointments with exterminators, plumbers, or other trades to show up at the house of some poor soul who had the unlucky occurrence of falling under our index finger as we poked randomly in the phone book.

One might think that making prank calls would be something you'd grow out of by the time you reached high school, but that was not the case with us. We actively made prank calls until whatever year caller ID was invented and found its way into most homes. Needless to say, the older we got, the more sophisticated our pranks became. But our best series of prank calls, to the same individual, went on randomly until we were in our early thirties.

While working at Thom McAn shoes in 1974, one of my prank-call cronies, who worked with me at the store, had a very unpleasant experience with a customer. While we constantly had unpleasant experiences with customers, this particular experience was over-the-top noteworthy and memorable. The customer actually ended up spitting on my friend; imagine a grown adult in a shoe store spitting on a seventeen-year-old kid making a $1.90 an hour because the youth dared to tell him he wasn't going to get his way.

This asshole paid for his bad behavior for the next fifteen years, as he was the recipient of an incessant stream of phone calls and hang ups at all hours of the night, any day of the week, any time of the year. Basically, any time it popped into my spat-upon friend's head to call, he'd call; mostly it would have been at a time when a phone call of any type, even a wrong number, would be unwelcome, say at 3:30 a.m. Unfortunately for the guy on the receiving end of the calls, my friend was a serious night owl.

Our favorite was the fake sales calls: "Yes, Mr. Spitter, this is Dick Cummings with Trojan Condoms, and I was wondering if you'd like a free sample of our XX-Small Sheepskin One-Eyed Snake Holsters?"

"They're free? Well … sure, I'll take a sample."

"All you need to do is answer a few questions about the type of condoms you currently use." (At this point, it would take an all but superhuman effort to stifle the laughter that would naturally want to erupt as you played this fool of a fish.)

Or, another …

"Hello, Mr. Spitter, this is Heywood Jablomie with Sears at Metcalf South, and we'd like to invite you to come by our Craftsman Tool department tomorrow for a free set of our Craftsman Abrasive Hole Reamers."

The greatest thing about this was that the guy was the utmost prank-call sucker of all time. Had we known about him when we were younger, we would have had him checking his refrigerator every day. We'd go through entire calls without him ever seeming to understand that he was being pranked. All we had to do was mention "free" something or other and he was putty in our hands. I honestly believe that he did show up at Sears on that particular Saturday asking for his free Craftsman Abrasive Hole Reamers, and then possibly he spat upon the poor sales guy when he was informed that they weren't giving away free tools that day. The coup de grâce, and final prank call to this individual, had both he and his wife on the phone participating in a market research study, for a solid twenty minutes, answering all sorts of ridiculous personal questions (including some red-faced queries into their sexual proclivities), with the payoff being a free cannister of Topsy's popcorn, which they could pick up the next day at the Topsy's at Metcalf South Shopping Center. And what made this call extra special was the fact that we recorded it and, to this day, we can still listen to it and fall rolling on the ground, right in the middle of a huge pile of unbridled mirth. Little did Mr. Spitter realize that one of the luckiest days of his life was the day that free caller ID was introduced. Nor did we realize that it was one of our darkest days.

※ ※ ※

I do not eat ketchup. I love both sugar and tomatoes, but for some reason, the mixture of the two is totally unappealing to me. Nothing ruins a good French fry or onion ring more than being slathered in that sweet, red, sugary goo. I realize I am in the minority. I remember liking ketchup as a kid, putting it on hamburgers, hot dogs, you name it; even French fries and onion rings. But in my eleventh year, on a blistering hot summer day, there occurred an event that turned me against that condiment for all of my subsequent days.

When we were kids, and we weren't privy to the economic struggles that adults encounter trying to house, educate, feed, and clothe kids — five kids, no less — we thought my father was a bit of a tightwad. (I now wonder and marvel at how, on one salary, he did what he did, and made us feel like we were rich — I'm certain if you're in my age group you wonder the same thing about your parents.) Tightwad or not, my father always did Christmas and vacations right. Regardless of how often he reminded us throughout the year that "We can't afford it!" or "You eat that cereal like you're the only kid in this family with a stomach!", he never disappointed us come Christmas and vacation time. Again, I don't know how my parents did it.

However, our summer vacation of 1967 was substandard compared to all of my previous vacations, certainly with regards to distance traveled and the lack of a body of water or an amusement park at the destination. I know now that this was because my parents had just finished building our final family house and cash was tight for necessities, which made it virtually nonexistent for discretionary spending on fun and frolic. Instead of a week at the beach or a Minnesota lakeshore, we went to visit family in St. Louis for a few days, then on to Chicago to visit the Museum of Science and Industry — an absolute requisite for a WWII-era mechanical engineer with three sons. (Still, broke or not, we took a vacation!)

Chicago was awesome, but it's St. Louis where my ketchup connection occurred. I was born in St. Louis, but moved to the OP at the age of three; I've got barely peripheral memories of St. Louis, at best. But my older brother and sister had some solid recollections of St. Louis, and some of their fondest memories involved the St. Louis Zoo. All kids love the zoo, and my eleven-year-old standard for a zoo was the Kansas City Zoo — damned fine by my estimation, but then it was all that I knew, and I was informed by my older siblings that the Kansas City Zoo was bupkis compared to the St. Louis Zoo. So needless to say, being a normal, zoo-loving kid, I was unconcerned about our truncated vacation and jazzed about a visit to what had been described to me, by reliable sources, as the mecca of all zoos.

The St. Louis Zoo was all that was promised, and far superior to Kansas City: an entire building dedicated to reptiles; a massive big-cat house; Phil, the poop-slinging gorilla; and an awesome walrus pool, to name but a few of the highlights. The lions seemed to roar louder, the seals appeared to swim faster, and the giraffes seemed to me at least ten feet taller than those that we had in Kansas City.

I was in heaven, but I was hungry; time for lunch at one of the crowded concessions stands. Picture a very hot summer day at the zoo, lots of people at the concession stand waiting in line, hungry for lunch: lots of kids, lots of dads — lots of hot, hungry, fussy kids; lots of hot, hungry, cranky dads. No matter to me, as I told my father what I wanted to eat, he got in line, and I moseyed around taking in the sights. There were perhaps twenty or thirty people huddled around the concession stand counter. It wasn't an organized queue as in an airport security checkpoint, back-and-forth fashion; it was kind of a mob at a counter — one of those situations in which the loudest and pushiest guy got waited on first. Those of us who aren't inclined to scream, push, and shove to get our way find nothing more obnoxious and offensive than those who are so inclined. This made those meek souls in the back of the line all the hotter, all the hungrier, and definitely a lot crankier as each minute passed. No worry for me, waltzing around in zoo la-la land, waiting patiently for my father to fight that crowd and bring me a burger with fries and a Coke to wash it down.

Oh, what's this, I asked myself, *an empty counter in the shade to lean against, with lots of napkins, plastic eating utensils, and mustard and ketchup packages? Maybe I'll just take a load off and lean here while I wait.* So, lean against the counter in the cool shade I did, and I can't say that what transpired next involved a similarly orderly, rational, internal discussion as to what I would or wouldn't do. We've all done or said things quickly or without thought that we've ended up regretting. Hopefully the inclination to commit these thoughtless, regrettable, spur-of-the-moment acts minimizes with age and experience. In fact, what I was about to do might be more explainable if I told you I was four years old when I did it, as opposed to being two years away from entering high school. Perhaps it was the midday summer heat, or the hunger, or the lingering euphoria of experiencing the walrus pool — I honestly can't say what drove me, in an unconscionable instant, to grab about a dozen of those ketchup packages, pile them carefully on the ground, and stomp upon them with all my might.

Every golfer knows what it feels like to connect with the "sweet spot" on a drive. It's a feeling so clean and so pure that the second it happens you know you've hit pay dirt. My size-six sneaker absolutely experienced that sweet-spot feeling as it laid into those twelve grounded ketchup packets that I'd fashioned into a compact little pyramid; really bad timing for that sweet-spot thing. Also, if there was ever an example of pressure on a tiny scale producing a force tenfold beyond what one would deem reasonable, this was that example.

I knew immediately that I had made a mistake. It was much like jabbing a rutting lion in the ass with a hot poker, having it turn to see what poked it, and standing there to face that angry beast — naked and unarmed. That hot, hungry, cranky crowd that was huddled, begging, growling, and fighting for food at the concession counter was, in an instant, diverted from their heat and hunger pangs, and left to concentrate on a blistering Heinz ketchup assault from their unprotected rear flank. All of the adults instantly snapped their heads forty-five degrees to their right to see just who in the hell might be responsible for this unprovoked attack, and there I stood, metaphorically naked and unarmed.

My action didn't kill anyone, or cause any actual physical harm, but the crowd looked as if lots of them were bleeding to death. The masterful distribution of the twelve ketchup packs — it wasn't a linear distribution, it was exponential — made it seem as if I'd spurted fifty gallons of ketchup at that crowd with a sophisticated piece of spray equipment; the kind of spray equipment after which a firefighter would lust. There were big gobs on this guy, fine spray on that guy, ribbons on the next one. And in 1960s fashion, all the dads had on collared, white short-sleeved shirts, and all the kids had crew cuts. I still have this vivid image of a dad on his knees, his white shirt splattered with ketchup, furiously wiping that sticky gunk from the side of his wailing five-year-old, crew-cutted son's head. He was cussing, and he looked as if he were struggling to decide between cleaning the mess from his son's head, or coming over to grab me by my ankles and throw me into the nearby lion's den.

As I was surveying the carnage I had wrought, I was truly in a state of awe over the damage inflicted by those twelve small packs of ketchup and one well-placed sneaker. For a very brief moment, I was actually starting to feel pride in what I had accomplished with such little effort and even less thought, and a slight smile started to break the plane of my awestruck visage. The smile quickly disappeared, as my father was on me in an instant. He grabbed me by the shoulders and started shaking me, saying, "What in the hell were you thinking? What made you do a stupid thing like that?" I was at a total loss for words, as to this day I still can't adequately answer either one of those questions, except with maybe a: "It seemed like a good idea at the time."

I remember a lot of the other dads saying things like "Kill the little bastard!" and "Let me have a crack at him!" I clearly recall that no one laughed it off, with the exception of my older brother, who was all but hysterical with laughter both at the magnitude of what I'd done and the prospect of watching me get my ass pounded in public. The rest of that unhappy crowd was going to have to walk around for the rest of a one-hundred-plus-degree day at the St. Louis Zoo with ketchup sprayed and splattered all over their clothes, crusted and cured in their hair and on their arms and legs, with the sweet, sickly smell of Heinz's finest permeating their nostrils into the late-afternoon hours, knowing that when they got home the only way they were going to be able to remove this mess from their skin was with a putty knife.

Much to the disappointment of the assembled throng, my father didn't put me over his knee and beat me within an inch of my life. In fact, only once did my father put me over his knee and spank me with his belt; he didn't have to spank me to get his point across, as the phrase "if looks could kill" was most certainly coined in the 1930s in Hannibal, Missouri, by someone who knew my father. He also sensed that the damage was done, and there was no point in using physical discipline as a teaching tool, him assuming that this was a one-shot deal and he didn't have to worry about me growing up and repeatedly wreaking havoc on innocents with condiment packages. And knowing my father as I do now, he probably thought it as funny as anything he'd seen in a while, and he knew his little display in front of the angry mob was all he needed to teach, and all I needed to learn, regarding the negative consequences of that once in a lifetime opportunity to plaster a crowd of people with ketchup packages.

When we caught up with my mother, I think she was probably more disappointed in me than was my father, especially when she saw the streaks of dried ketchup that emblazoned my father's entire right side, as the fine art of doing laundry expertly was always first and foremost in my mother's mind. For the next few days, out of nowhere, Mom would pop out with a "What on earth would possess you to do such a thing?" as if it was on her mind eternally, worrying that what I'd done to those innocent bystanders might be a precursor to me selecting the career path of a homicidal maniac.

I have to admit, on more than one occasion since the ketchup incident at the St. Louis Zoo, I've been at an airport, or a McDonald's, or the ballpark, and I've leaned against that same type of condiment counter, looked out at the unsuspecting crowd, and then glanced down at my heavy-soled, size-eleven clodhoppers and thought, *Nah ... better not.*

One of the highlights of the summer for me and my immediate group of low-level reprobate neighborhood buddies was our annual staging of the backyard carnival, held for the purpose of raising money for the Muscular Dystrophy Association. The nexus for this idea was spawned from the annual Jerry Lewis MDA Labor Day Telethon, and further promoted in Kansas City and the OP by a local television personality, Torey Southwick, and his hand puppet sidekick, Ol' Gus. Torey and Ol' Gus were on TV every afternoon when we arrived home from school, showing old black-and-white cartoons, mixed in amongst the occasional guest and folksy chatter over the back fence between Torey and Ol' Gus.

In the spring of each year, Torey and Ol' Gus would start promoting the idea of holding these backyard fundraisers, and assist by providing any interested party an official "Torey & Ol' Gus MDA Backyard Carnival Kit," which you received at no cost by sending in a postcard with your name and address. The kit contained promotional posters, which you would tack up on your local cancer-causing, creosote-coated wooden utility poles, event and game tickets, ideas for games and contests, and an envelope in which you could deposit the revenue from your event and send it straight in to the national office of the Muscular Dystrophy Association. The whole affair was a very noble pursuit, the sort of which seemed to be more prevalent back in our day.

Every year, the postcard would be sent in to Torey & Ol' Gus, and the carnival packet would be eagerly anticipated, as every year there were new designs and additional froufrou. The carnival date would be set, the games would be planned, and the signs would be tacked up throughout Grasmere Acres, Apple Valley, and Nall Hills. My mother would take us to U.S. Toy, located under a bridge near 85th and Troost (right across the street from the original Stroud's Fried Chicken!), where we would pick out scads of little plastic trinkets to give away as prizes for winners of the "Wheel Of Fortune" game, or Lawn Bowling Alley, or any other number of games that usually involved little neighborhood kids throwing things at some sort of a target.

There was only one small, delinquent hitch with our backyard Muscular Dystrophy fundraisers. I recall us occasionally siphoning some of the earnings before sending the money we raised from the fundraiser in to Torey, Ol' Gus, Jerry Lewis, or the poor children who were afflicted with Muscular Dystrophy. It wasn't ever a lot of money, certainly not enough to qualify for fraud on any illegal scale, but us keeping some of the cash also certainly wasn't being done in accordance with the spirit that Torey & Ol' Gus intended. I'm sure I've paid for this malfeasance somewhere along the line, or may yet ultimately have to answer for it. I know that in my later teen years I would pledge twenty-five dollars towards MDA during the Jerry Lewis telethon, and I've also dropped numerous dollar bills, dimes, and quarters into firefighters' boots after being accosted at traffic lights on Labor Day weekend — enough so that I've hopefully paid back my transgression in spades.

(As an aside, I recall the final year of my participation in the backyard carnival, we earned a decent amount of money, and through a friend of a friend, we were invited to present the money on local television during a noon-time news and variety show hosted by Jack Cafferty, known as *Cafferty & Friends*. I was way too old, and way too cool, to participate in such an affair, and instead was represented by my younger brother and one of his close friends. As Jack Cafferty called my brother and his friend to the front of the studio crowd for the check presentation, he asked for what charity was the money raised, and my brother, obviously nervous, with a passel of big medical terms swimming around in his head, proudly blurted out, "We've raised this money to help all of the children who suffer from Muscular Psoriasis!")

While most of our intentions in raising the money came from our pure hearts, our methods for raising the money were forged from deep within a devious den in our souls. The Apple Valley Dungeon of Doom Spookhouse started out innocently enough as a trip through T-Gray's basement, the young customer being blindfolded and taken from one scary station to the next. On a table sat a bowl with a half dozen wet, peeled green grapes, which participants would be asked to pick up, and then learn that they were holding Frankenstein's monster's eyeballs. Or they'd stick their hands into a large bowl of cold oatmeal, and find out that it wasn't really oatmeal, it was actually poor old Frankenstein's monster's brains. We'd have them stand in front of a desk fan, and tell them they were outside the entrance to the haunted Cave of the Ghost Winds. A feather duster was brushed across their arms and then over their blindfolded faces, and we'd shriek, "OH MY

GOD, you just got attacked by the giant Death Spider of Nallwood!" All in all, it was pretty lame stuff, especially considering we charged a quarter for it (and that was relatively heavy coin at the time), but the kids seemed to enjoy it, certainly more than we did, as after about the fifth customer, we started getting bored with it. Unfortunately, we had kids lined up outside waiting their turn to get in, and there was no turning back. Possibly it was the large sign, an impressive piece of marketing brilliance, that proclaimed, "YOU MUST BE 6 YEARS OF AGE TO ENTER! NO REFUNDS FOR BEING SCARED TO DEATH!"

T-Gray's older brother, whom we called "Coach," pulled a pretty good one out of his pocket to spice up the festivities. He came up with the idea of putting these blindfolded youngsters into a Red Flyer wagon, telling them to hang on for dear life, and pulling them around the basement at breakneck speed. So what if one or two of them fell out, smashing their bodies as they rolled across the concrete basement floor. That wasn't nearly as bad as the poor kid whose forehead slammed into the edge of the Ping-Pong table, sending him somersaulting backwards out of the wagon, giving him a concussion-inducing knot on the back of his head to match the black-and-blue welt that was quickly forming on the front of his young skull. It took us a few minutes to get him calmed down before we sent him out to his mom, crying to the point of hyperventilation with tears streaming down his face, as we barked out to assembled line, "Alright, kids, who's next to visit the Dungeon of Doom and ride the death-defying Roller Ruby (the on-the-spot name for the Red Flyer, which more accurately should have been referred to as the Wagon of Near Maiming.) That'll be twenty-five cents!"

The danger didn't stop there. The desk fan that served as the entrance to The Cave of the Ghost Winds quickly turned into The Cave of the Haunted Seas when one of us poured a cup of water into the blades, spraying and soaking the poor little six-year-old whose mother had unwittingly coughed up a quarter to have her child be tortured. But it gets even worse. One of us discovered that the electric fan, sitting in a puddle of water on the table, also gave off a mild electric shock when we had the kids put their hands onto the wet surface of the table, they now being visitors to the Lair of the Man-Eating Electric Eel! ZAAPPP!

In spite of all the physical mayhem that was being perpetrated upon these innocents, most of them exiting the Dungeon of Doom in a state of near hysteria, some crying, and a few exhibiting symptoms of mild shock, the line to pay a quarter for the privilege of putting themselves in serious harm's way didn't diminish. Torey & Ol' Gus would have been impressed!

Outside in the backyard, safely away from the Dungeon of Doom, we had one low-rent thrill ride, which we called The Himalaya. In our day, we had these four-seat metal teeter-totter sort of things, where everyone had a seat, and a handle, which they pumped back and forth to make it spin round and round at dizzying speeds. They were common in the backyards of the '60s, along with swing sets and jungle gyms — all of this acceptable stuff for kids to occupy themselves with before the advent of one out of every three smart kids going to law school. Our engineering fathers contrived this sort of entertainment for their children before their children shunned engineering school in exchange for the less mathematically challenging, more profitable, education of tort law, from which they would profit by suing their mechanically clever, mathematically inclined progenitors for creating backyard hazards.

What made The Himalaya unique, and worth spending cash on for the child of the '60s to ride, was that the contraption was missing one of the four legs. So it was like an off-balance, herky-jerky, teeter-totter, octopus sort of ride, which was especially herky-jerky when not all four of the riders were in the same weight class. Put one fat kid, or one really skinny kid, on one of the four seats, and this little metal back-and-forth, round and round contraption spun and bucked like a drunken donkey on speed. Most people would have thrown this broken plaything into the dumpster, but we featured it in our backyard fundraiser, not for the Muscular Dystrophy afflicted, but to challenge and potentially maim the healthy children in the OP. Upon reflection, it now seems fittingly warped.

The final bit of hooliganism was a little more subtle than the aforementioned I'll-pay-you-to-abuse-me sorts of entertainment options for our patrons. These were the games of chance, and like many games of chance found on actual carnival midways, they were rigged in favor of the hooligans. The last year we held the carnival (we would have been eighth graders, thirteen or fourteen years of age), we imported an outsider to help us with the production, one Paul Morton, he being a youth who was born to the con. Paul was one of those kids that everyone knew somewhere along the line in their lives — he wasn't hard-core delinquent, but he was constantly straddling the line of legitimacy as far as activities that parents might consider unwholesome.

Paul's contribution to the carnival was a few games of chance, the first being the "Wheel of Fortune." Participants would put a ticket, or multiple tickets, on a strip of numbers, one through ten, and hope that when the wheel was spun, it would land on their chosen number, much like a roulette table in a casino. The prizes were displayed behind the wheel, and they were of a much higher stead than the plastic spider rings, or the woven Chinese finger traps that were purchased at U.S. Toy. There were some large stuffed animals, a nice flashlight, and even a transistor radio, all supplied by Mr. Morton, the game's nefarious designer. Paul could have safely offered up a prize of one million dollars to the winning ticket, as the numbers one through ten were on the board, but nowhere on the spinning wheel were the numbers one through ten. The wheel included fractions, numbers with decimal points, a few ten-digit numbers, and even one space that simply read "Infinity." These were little kids, and the concept of the board corresponding to the wheel was lost on them, and our mothers were never involved enough in the minutia of our lives at that point that they would have picked up on this blatant scam. But one mother — she being the mother of my friend who ended up becoming a United States senator — *she* was paying attention, and she shut down the old "Wheel of Fortune," lest we got raided and busted for fraud by the OP Bunco Squad, potentially damaging her son's chances of growing up to become a United States senator, or at least an honest United States senator.

Paul's second contribution was the Duck Pond, a small plastic wading pool that had twenty or so rubber ducks floating in it; if you picked a rubber duck with a star on the bottom, you won a prize. You guessed it. None of the rubber ducks had a star on the bottom. And Paul's coup de grâce was the midway classic, "Topple the Milk Bottles with a Baseball" game, except instead of using milk bottles, he had ten empty tin cans stacked in a pyramid, in a large box, about twenty feet from the throwing line. Fortunately for us, most little kids couldn't throw a ball accurately from a distance of twenty feet. But in the rare case that they would have been able to, they wouldn't have been able to knock those cans over with a bulldozer, let alone the Wiffle ball that the preteen contestants would be throwing, as Paul Morton all but welded the cans together, and weighted them down by filling them full of some sort of lead shot.

In spite of all the sleight of hand and near death by electrocution, those little neighborhood kids who weren't in tears left the carnival with smiles on their faces and the occasional plastic trinket in their pockets. When your normal summer day as a child in the OP involved sitting around waiting for something — anything — to happen, the Greatest Show in Grasmere Acres had to have been one of the highlights of your summer, as it certainly was one of ours.

So, the next time you see your children, or grandchildren, with their noses buried in some sort of technology device, or find them lounging slothfully on a couch playing *Fortnite*, or binge-watching *Game of Thrones*, don't despair. For it is these soul-sapping, mind-numbing, modern-day accoutrements to life that may be saving this new generation of earthly inhabitants from an early demise at the hands of the Man-Eating Electric Eel.

※ ※ ※

Speaking of Paul Morton, the only bit of delinquency that bordered upon the hard-core, i.e., harm to humans or property, occurred with his assistance and, quite frankly, was of his device and execution. We all look back on things we've done in our past lives that have given us heartburn; I've chronicled more than a few. But this stunt could still, to this day, maybe get me arrested for assault. I'm hoping, and assuming, that there is a statute of limitations on assault crimes, as I will plead this should I get picked up by the OP Police Department after publishing this book.

There was a social prank in the mid-1970s that involved smashing pies in the face of "the man." It was a little like Guy Fawkes without firebombs, but armed with coconut crème pies. The perpetrators masked themselves, and sort of chicken-shittedly, ANTIFA-like, accosted people that they thought were moneyed, privileged souls that needed to be taken down. The irony of this was that I was the last soul on Earth that thought innocents, regardless of their income or social standing, needed to be harassed. But for some strange reason, I bought into Paul Morton's need to smash a pie into some unsuspecting adult's face.

Pappy's BBQ restaurant was on the lowest level of Metcalf South Shopping Center, on the southernmost end, near the exit doors that were bordered by the Sears store. It was a wonderful place, where you could enjoy a delicious smoked turkey sandwich, with a side of onion rings that were so perfectly prepared, crispy, and crunchy that they'd all but chip your teeth if you weren't careful. They also served Coors on tap, in mugs that were iced to a state that would induce tears in your eyes as one was set before you with that sandwich and those perfect onion rings. The meal only cost a poor, young shoe dog on his lunch break four bucks, less a tip, to savor this feast.

The proprietor of this little slice of heaven was a man named Reed Austin, aka Pappy. He was from all appearances to a young eighteen-year-old, a grumpy, dumpy, old white guy; black horn-rimmed glasses; sporting a Marine-style buzz flattop haircut, that hair white as the OP winter snow. He hung out at the bar, chatting with the old-timers who planted themselves on stools sipping beer and smoking cigarettes throughout the day. (Imagine this happening at a shopping mall today. Imagine there actually being a shopping mall today!) Us kids buying lunch were but an annoying encumbrance to him as he held court over the OP locals that clogged up his barstools, sipping their ice-cold Coors whilst swapping stories and telling lies.

For whatever reason, at that particular time, I found him to be an irritable old curmudgeon, yet someone who was a fairly high-profile irritable old curmudgeon. Thus, when Paul Morton discussed his plan of "pie-ing" a deserving, semi-high-profile, cranky old bastard, Reed Austin immediately came to my mind. I'm still not entirely sure why. He'd never done anything to me other than serve me good food and take my money, a quid pro quo of natural order.

The attack was to be on an innocuous Wednesday during the lunch hour. Paul Morton would supply the pie and, masked, would walk into a crowded lunchtime Pappy's BBQ and, without any provocation, slam a pie into poor Pappy's face as he lorded over his restaurant and bar. We actually told some associates, Thom McAn employees, who told numerous other mall employees, that this was indeed going to happen, and the place was packed to the gills. The poor onion-ring fryer was smoking hot, gasping for air to keep up with demand, clueless as to why this random Wednesday would have brought out such a crowd.

I was giddy with the thought of this, but wanted no part in the actual assault. My job was to drive Paul Morton, drop him off, park right outside the mall entrance, and wait with the passenger-side car door open. I even chicken-pooped out on driving my own car, borrowing a car from another friend, an unwilling and unapproving accomplice in this insanity.

It all went down pretty bang-bang. Paul Morton leaves the car, pie in hand, and heads into the mall. Two short minutes later, he's running out the mall door, jumping into the open car door, and telling me to "Hit it!" Right behind him was Pappy's son, Arnold, who ran to the driver's side of the car (not my car!) and savagely ripped the windshield wiper from its moors, then backed away, holding the limp and impotent windshield wiper, looking disgusted, as I drove that car (not my car!) fast as hell out of there.

I was told by witnesses to the affair that the masked Paul Morton walked into the crowded, dark restaurant, went up to Pappy and yelled, "This is vengeance, courtesy of the Sons of Loki!", smashed the pie into half of Pappy's face, and ran from the restaurant, leaving a crowd of people stunned as to what they'd just witnessed. Even the people who we'd prepped for the event were gob smacked. Who in the hell were the Sons of Loki? That was a classic Paul Morton touch.

Forty-five years later, in retrospect, I am stunned to believe I had any part in any such event. This makes shooting flaming arrows at my wooden roof, at a wasp's nest, during an OP summer heatstroke seem logical. I owe it up to the fact that we all have that one friend, most probably a fringe friend, that pushes us to a place where we don't normally go or belong. This degenerate behavior doesn't come from our core but is a residue of living vicariously through those who we aren't, be it a scruffy kid from Tulsa trying too hard to make a first impression, or a teenage all but grifter we happened upon, growing up in the OP.

Growing Up with Raging Hormones IN THE OP

WARNING: GRAPHIC LANGUAGE
To this point, this book has contained very little profanity. All that it has, has been used out of necessity to the plot of the story or in direct quotes. This is also the case with the forthcoming chapter, as the bad language is not only germane to the story, it is essential to accurately describing the subject of the story, which is raging, uncontrollable teenage hormones. I apologize for this, as I am very selective in my life about using bad language, and one of these words, I don't ever use at all. I'll warn you: it is the C-word. If you are offended by this, I suggest you skip to the next chapter. I'm being serious.

You would most likely need to be a male to fully understand this; I don't believe this particular affliction is suffered by females, or certainly wasn't by any females that I knew at the time. When most young boys start sniffing around the doors of preteen adolescence, both their minds and bodies are, out of nowhere, bombarded by overwhelming sexual desires. Sex is all they think about, talk about, read about, and dream about. They'd risk just about anything for a peek down a woman's blouse, or a brief glance up a skirt; even the outline of a bra strap on the back of a burgeoning seventh-grade classmate was enough to shorten the breath at the thought of what lay gently ensconced within the cups of that expertly engineered latex and cotton contraption. I was one such young boy, and maybe you were, too.

If so, you'd think about sex so much that you'd actually go to the time and effort of sending one or two of your hard-earned dollars (allowance back then was twenty-five cents a week — at least that's what it was at my house) to some company found in the back of some comic book for a pair of X-Ray glasses, with an advertising tag line of '*Is that really their body you see under their clothes?*' No, it wasn't.

You'd think about sex so much that you eagerly await the monthly delivery — you know it to the day — of the *National Geographic*, quickly scouring each issue for articles on recently discovered primitive native tribes. If that issue actually had an article on a recently discovered, primitive, very possibly NAKED! native tribe, that particular issue probably never made it on the bookshelf in the family room — the bookshelf that contained all of the past *National Geographic*s, all the way back to 1959, in chronological order, save for a missing random month here and there. After *National Geographic* being your first introduction to naked breasts and the female body, imagine the level of heart-stopping excitement that awaited you when you came across your first *Playboy*, and you discovered that not all female breasts look like tube socks.

You'd think about sex so much that in seventh grade, the grade in which your high standing on the popularity chart becomes eminently important, you'd befriend the biggest nerd in the class when you found out he had unfettered access to his dad's massive collection of *Playboy* magazines — and his mom didn't care that you sat around looking at them. What? Were these people from Mars?

You'd think about sex so much that even hearing a dirty word in a song would be a potential source of titillation. (Imagine today, being titillated by hearing the F-word in a song; good gracious, if that were the case, we'd all be walking around eternally like billy goats in heat.) This happened to me in seventh grade, 1968, when three or four of us spent the night at Mike McGinley's house, sitting around a small, single-speaker portable record player, listening over and over and over again to a 45-rpm record, the Cream song "White Room." It was the only song we listened to that night, and we probably listened to it twenty times, maybe thirty times. No question, it was and still is a tremendous song, but twenty to thirty times in a row? We listened to it over and over and over again not so much because we liked it, but because we wanted to hear the part where Jack Bruce sings, "I'll wait … to fuck you, when the trains … come back." That's correct. We thought the lyrics were, "I'll wait to fuck you … ." We weren't one hundred percent sure that's what he was saying, but we were pretty sure, and that's why we listened to it over and over and over again, to convince ourselves that we were actually hearing the F-word, in a song, on the radio. If he wasn't saying the F-word, what else on earth could it be? And every time Jack Bruce sang that line, we'd giggle, swoon, groan, thinking, *Oh baby, he's waiting to have sex with her. How awesome is that?*

This is true. About forty-five years later, I'm driving back to the office after having dropped a fellow employee at the airport, and I'm listening to my iPod, as is my usual custom when driving alone in the car. I always have the iPod on shuffle, so I can go from hearing a movement from a Mahler Symphony, to "Red Rubber Ball" by the Cyrkle, to Van Morrison mumbling and wailing something about listening to a lion. On this particular day, up pops "White Room," and as I'm half listening, half thinking about the rest of my day, and absentmindedly concentrating on the road that lay before me, it suddenly hits me as if the sky had opened up and all of humanity's heretofore unknown mysteries were revealed to me:

Oh My God, he's saying "I WAIT IN THE QUEUE!!" In the QUEUE!!!! Not "I wait to fuck you," but, "I wait in the Queue"!!!

Forty-five years after sitting on the floor listening to that song, over and over and over and over again, it finally dawned on me that Jack Bruce wasn't waiting to have sex, he was simply waiting in line for a train. What a disappointment!

It was also in seventh grade when I, and most of the rest of Curé of Ars Catholic Grade School, was exposed to one of, if not the most, vulgar words in the English language; it is considered as such still to this day. It's even worse than the F-word. It is the C-word.

The year would have been 1968, and the month would have been October. We were in the midst of a presidential campaign. The candidates were Richard Nixon, the eventual winner, and Hubert Humphrey, the Minnesotan who was vice president under Lyndon Johnson; both were vying for the office after Lyndon Johnson stepped down from his single term as president. While not yet passionately politically aware, we were certainly of an age when we knew who was running, and we would have had a preference, solidly based upon the preference of our parents. (It wasn't until college that our preference would possibly be the polar opposite of the political preference of our parents.)

There were two seventh and two eighth grade classes at Curé, both containing approximately thirty students. Our four classrooms were all on the upper floor of the school, with a common hallway, across the hall from the nun's convent — that most mysterious of places on earth, a place into which no kid had ever stepped foot. Not only did the seventh and eighth graders share a floor and a hallway, but they also shared the four homeroom teachers for all of their subjects. Sister Vivian was the math teacher, Miss Roschitz taught English, Sister Mary Richard taught religion and science, and Sister Dorothy taught geography and history. I remember Sister Dorothy as very young and sweet — certainly sweet for a nun — with dark hair and those bluish horn-rimmed glasses that many females wore back in the '60s. I believe 1968 to also be the year that the Sisters of Saint Joseph, the order that served northeastern Kansas, got rid of the old black penguin habits and began wearing regular street clothes.

What I will reveal next speaks to the wonderful level of naivete that many of us possessed way back when. Many of my Curé of Ars contemporaries will back me up on this story, as it now seems so fantastic that it is hard to believe it occurred.

Sister Dorothy, as the geography and history teacher, wanted to get her eighth-grade students involved in the current election. She encouraged the students to decorate the rooms with signs — hand drawn and colored; or actual political yard signs, bumper stickers, and such — for the candidates of their choice. Both eighth grades rooms were quickly decorated with "NIXON'S THE ONE!" or "HUMPHREY IS GREAT IN '68!" There were also signs for the lesser congressional and senate races, governor, attorney general, etc. You have to realize that things were typically so strict in our school that this short-lived moratorium on decorum — i.e., the ability to plaster stuff, random and pell-mell, all over the classrooms — was met with universal glee amongst all of the students. Two eighth-grade boys (one of whose name I remember, but will spare him the indignity) took the "random and pell-mell" thing to a whole new level, a level that would even be considered cutting edge and shocking by today's anything-goes standards. These two lads, with seemingly no regard for their lives or limbs considering the fact that they were dealing with nuns, invented two presidential candidates, actually telling Sister Dorothy that they were independent write-in candidates. And back to the surreal level of naivete, she let this pass through without qualification. The two candidates for president and vice president that the boys were touting, and had plastered signs of support and advertisement all over Sister Dorothy's classroom for, were Harry Wong for president, and Mary C-word for vice president. I'm not making this up. (FYI, "wong" was a slang term for a penis back then; I haven't much heard it lately, except amongst the few remaining friends of mine from Curé of Ars, who still refer to a penis as nothing but a "wong.")

That's correct. Signs were quickly produced by many of the students and taped to every available bit of wall space, desk space, in the bathrooms, and in the hallway: "VOTE FOR WONG AND C-WORD!" or "WONG AND C-WORD FOR ALL OF US!" or "WHO WANTS WONG & C-WORD? WE ALL WANT WONG & C-WORD!!"

This "Wong & C-Word" hysteria — and a hysteria it was — immediately caught fire with most of the students. I can honestly say that I'd never heard either of those words before, and I had no idea what either of them meant when I first heard them. This was most probably the case with the great majority of the rest of the seventh and eighth graders at Curé of Ars, but, by golly, we all learned lickety-split what they meant, quickly exposing 120 puritan-eared students to a whole new level of vulgarity. Imagine our shock, and then our unbridled delight, when we heard our teachers stand in front of a classroom and *say out loud* things like, "Who are Wong and C-Word? I've never heard of them!" or "Well if you all are so much for Wong and C-Word, then I will be as well!" It was beyond imaginable to us previously innocent little Catholic scholars to have that sort of filth uttered out loud, *by our teachers!* And to add to the hilarity, after the teacher would make some sort of reference to Wong and C-Word, most of the males in the classroom would begin to chant "WONG & C-WORD! WONG & C-WORD! WONG & C-WORD!" as the teacher smiled and went along, clapping her hands in time to the obscene chant, happy to see that her students were so involved in their civic duty of supporting a presidential candidate.

It lasted for two days. We never heard how the four teachers found out that not only were Wong & C-Word not legitimate write-in candidates for the United States presidency, but they were actually fictional people named after really filthy words. Hell hath seen no fury like that which discharged from the formerly sweet Sister Dorothy. I was unlucky (or lucky?) enough to be in her room for geography when the word came down. We were sitting in the classroom, most probably casually discussing Wong & C-Word while waiting for Sister Dorothy to enter and begin our daily geography lesson, when in she flew, in a blind rage, leaping at the walls and tearing down all of the carefully crafted and artfully decorated WONG & C-WORD FOR US!! signs. It was a frightening sight to see, this diminutive nun, with her blue horn-rimmed glasses, behind which now showed eyes that were glowing like fiery coals, her spittle raining through the air as she barked and fumed mostly gibberish that had been forged from a violent place in the depths of her soul, spinning and whirling like the cartoonish Tasmanian devil, flying about the room as she ripped, tore, threw, and trashed every bit of paper or cardboard that contained those vile words. I'm now certain that most of her inner rage stemmed from the realization that she and her cohorts had been so badly duped by a bunch of godless, evil, little heathens.

The two campaign managers for Wong & C-Word were expelled. As for the rest of us, there wasn't much they could do except fume at us. For all they knew we were just as innocent as they: "Honest Sister Dorothy, I thought Wong & C-Word really were running for President! Just like you!"

One great thing that Catholic schools had over public schools was Holy Days of Obligation holidays, i.e., random days out of school in addition to the regular public school holidays such as Thanksgiving, Christmas, and Spring Break. Catholic school kids got the day after Halloween off, as that was All Saints Day; December 8th was an off day, as that was the Feast of the Immaculate Conception; Holy Thursday, Good Friday, and Easter Monday were all off days. It used to drive my public school friends crazy, especially the day after Halloween holiday, they having to trudge off to school the next morning, their brains still racing from an overdose of caffeinated corn syrup and cocoa.

It was on one of those random day-off holidays in eighth grade that my mother drove four of us to downtown Kansas City for a day of absolutely-no-good troublemaking fun. I'm still to this day surprised that I talked her into letting us wander around downtown for the day, as this was 1969, and there was absolutely nothing of substance for thirteen-year-old males to do in downtown Kansas City, certainly from the point of view of my mother, anyway. But for the four thirteen-year-old boys who chose to celebrate the Feast of the Immaculate Conception in and around the vicinity of 12th Street and Grand Avenue, downtown was loaded with opportunities for potentially seeing naked women, and, by golly, there was no better reason on earth to put our lives in harm's way on the mean streets of downtown Kansas City, Missouri.

My mother dropped us off at 12th Street and Grand Avenue, that being the site of Wonderland Arcade, which was one of our primary destinations but not *the* primary destination. Within seconds after my mom's white Pontiac Tempest disappeared from sight, we shot westward like cattle out of the chute, up a gentle incline towards the filthiest block in downtown KC, which was 12th Street between Wyandotte and Central. (This section of real estate is now home to the Marriott Hotel, which is directly across from Barney Allis Plaza and the Municipal Auditorium.)

During the 1930s and 1940s, there were actually some respectable jazz clubs along this stretch, but by the late 1960s, many would claim that it had degenerated to a block full of seedy strip clubs and dive bars. The four of us eighth graders did not consider these 1969 12th Street tenants as a degeneration of property; rather, we were walking as fast as our skinny little shanks would carry us towards what we believed was Mecca — The Jewel Box, The Kitty Kat Club, The Boom-Boom Room, and, the shining star of the bunch, The Folly Burlesque Theater. As all of the other aforementioned establishments served alcohol, we knew there wasn't a chance in hell we'd be able to sneak into any of them, but the Folly was simply an old theater with live strippers and stag movies. In retrospect, our plan for getting four eighth-grade boys into a building that required its patrons to be eighteen years of age was a thousand bricks shy of a thousand-brick building. But at the time, our clear thinking was completely obfuscated by the one in a million chance of actually getting to watch a live woman take off her clothes. To us the plan was totally plausible, if not teetering upon the brink of brilliance.

There was one in our group, Paul Morton, who was actually fourteen years of age, and he was more than a little ahead of the rest of us in terms of his pursuit of puberty. His voice had already changed and he was starting to get underarm hair and BO; but the big kicker was him actually having noticeable facial hair, enough so that he'd already started shaving, maybe once or twice. If you didn't know any better, you'd see him on the street and think that maybe he was possibly sixteen years old! To us, Paul looked so much older that we thought the chances were pretty solid that Paul wouldn't get carded when he went to buy four tickets to get us all into the theater. He'd simply buy the tickets, hand them to each of us individually, and one by one we'd head through the turnstile on our way into heaven, the ticket taker just assuming that if we had tickets in our possession, we must have already been carded and, therefore, were legit. The remaining three of us positioned ourselves on the Central Avenue side of the Folly while Paul walked slowly to the box office, his head looking straight down at the sidewalk, all of us hoping beyond hope that the ticket seller would be asleep at the switch and not bother to question this all but faceless, deep-voiced little kid who wanted to buy, not one, but four tickets to the noon matinee nudiefest.

As you can easily predict, it was less than one minute before Paul Morton was around that corner, back amongst us, with not one lousy ticket to the Folly Burlesque in his hand. As taking advantage of Paul's jump start on puberty was our most solid plan, one that we'd actually worked on and rehearsed for a few weeks, we decided it was probably smart to wait another five years until our eighteenth birthdays before attempting to buy tickets to see live strippers in downtown KC.

The next stop on our quest for filth was east, back down on 12th Street, at the Time to Read Bookstore — at that time the most notorious porn parlor in Kansas City. Time to Read was a long, narrow store filled with legitimate books, mostly paperback, every magazine imaginable, a massive collection of comic books, sports and movie periodicals, and newspapers from around the globe. But the real reason most anyone went into Time to Read was for the long aisle on the right-hand side of the store, the aisle that had a small, hand-printed white cardboard sign hanging over the entrance that read, "YOU MUST BE 18 YEARS OLD TO ENTER." As previously chronicled, we weren't eighteen, and we couldn't enter, but we could saunter back and forth in front of the entrance to that magical aisle, look down the aisle to catch glimpses of magazine covers that featured bare-breasted women with starred nipples, and hope to spot the Holy Grail of puberty-fueled fantasies, that being a naked woman with her legs spread open, the pay dirt part being covered with a large black circle. It didn't matter, as just thinking about what was underneath that circle was more than enough to turn us into hyperactive little horndogs. Unfortunately, it wasn't but ten minutes into our visit that one of the crusty old curmudgeons that worked at Time to Read figured out what we were up to and gave us the bum's rush.

Next stop on our route was Wonderland Arcade, at the corner of 12th Street and Grand Avenue. This was one of the coolest places on the face of the earth at that time in my life, as there wasn't much I liked more than playing pinball, Skee-Ball, and all and any of the other arcade games — games that predated video games such as Pac-Man and Space Invaders, which came to being when I was in college. The four of us plowed through Wonderland like a beaver through a rotting tree, moving from machine to machine, slamming dimes and quarters into the slots with reckless abandon. We'd been there maybe thirty minutes when one of us got the idea to get our pictures taken in one of those old four-for-a-quarter picture booths. The same one of us then had a better idea — let's get in the photo booth and take pictures of us all mooning the camera. (Mooning was just starting to come into vogue as a means of counterculture expression.) This stunt now seems logistically impossible to me, as those booths were barely big enough for two people, with nothing but a small, circular, swivel chair to sit upon. But, honest to God, we worked it to where we were all able to drop our drawers, drop in a quarter, and get four pictures of four young butts.

We exited the booth, and as we were waiting for the pictures to develop and come out of the dispenser, one of the employees came up and started chatting with us. Like the man at Time to Read, he also was cut from the cloth of crusty curmudgeonliness, but was a little friendlier than the guy that hustled us out of the porn aisle. The pictures are dispensed, and the employee retrieves them, casually glancing down at them as he's handing them to us.

"Why ... I don't know what happened, boys, but none of these pictures came out very good. Get back in there and I'll put in another quarter for you."

So back in the booth we went, kind of half snickering and half holding our breaths, but this time we just took pictures of our faces — sticking out our tongues, crossing our eyes, that sort of thing. It was maybe after the third flashbulb exploded that we heard from outside the booth, "HEY! ... *Wait a minute! ... These are pictures of your BUTTS!*"

With that, the screen flew open, and that kind old curmudgeon turned into a really cranky old curmudgeon. "You boys get out here, NOW." He literally chased us out of the store, banishing us from the place where we had intended to spend the better part of our day.

We found ourselves standing on the corner of 12th and Grand on a cold, damp December religious holiday, barely one full hour into our eight-hour day of downtown debauchery. There was no place else for us to go, there was nothing else for us to do, and there wasn't a naked lady in sight.

Everything I ever learned about sex, I learned on the mean streets of The OP from my older brother and his friends. My father never sat me down and gave me the facts-of-life talk. He did take me to a one-night sex education class at Village Presbyterian, where all of the fathers went in one room (probably to drink, smoke, and play cards) and all of the young males went into another room, where we were given a small paperback and an accompanying talk by a lay teacher. Of course, the book was scarcely in our hands before every single one of us little perverts were quickly thumbing through it looking for pictures of naked women. There were none to be found; just some drawings of things like ovaries and fallopian tubes. What a letdown!

In my freshman year of high school, in religion class, there was a four-day lesson on sex education, given by a Jesuit priest, Father Eugene Martens, who more than likely had never had a sexual encounter in his life. This would be a little like a lifelong vegan teaching a class on the finer points of gutting a pig. I remember very little about the class, but I do vividly recall him saying, "During the sex act, the woman will lay quietly, acting as soft and gentle as a lamb, while the man will become loud and excitable, and explode like a string of firecrackers!" I'm not making that up; he actually said that. Turns out he was right.

Even into high school, I was so naïve about sex that I still believed God would impregnate women. Oh, I knew about sexual intercourse, as Father Martens had discussed that act in clinical detail, but I thought that some babies were made through sexual intercourse, while others were products of divine impregnation. I remember having a discussion with my close friend and pyro buddy, T. Gray, asking, "Do you think your parents had sex to have you, or do you think you are a God baby?" This whacked notion came from television shows that I'd seen in which the male character in a sitcom comes home from work and his wife excitedly bursts out with, "Guess what, dear? I'm pregnant!!!" My reasoning was that surely if you'd had sex it would be zero surprise that you'd be pregnant. Having sex equaled having a baby. You'd only be surprised if you woke up one morning and found yourself pregnant by the hand of God; then and only then would you blurt out to your husband in an amazed and excited fashion, "Surprise, dear, *I'm pregnant!!*"

I also for a short while thought that the term "pubic hair" was actually "public hair." It was one of those instances of your eyes playing tricks on you, seeing something as you thought it was versus what it actually was. Can you imagine being so stupid as to think that hair that was in the most private of places would be referred to as "public"? And it turns out I wasn't the only idiot on the block, as one of my best friends, who has gone on in life to reach a nationally renowned pinnacle of intellectual success as a real-live, honest-to-God United States senator, also thought the word read as public. I remember having discussions with him about this, wondering who on earth came up with the idea to refer to the hair around your privates as public. "Maybe it's some sort of a deal like it's an oxymoron on purpose, like they were trying to be funny and went out of their way to call it the opposite of what it is." And one day, a little like the "I wait in the queue" moment (except this happened way before I was sixty years old), I was more than likely reading something mildly pornographic, when I saw the word and it hit me — *BAM*! — "It's PUBIC, not PUBLIC! PUBIC! PUBIC! PUBIC!" And just like that, the mystery of my life's greatest oxymoron was solved.

It saddens me a little that my following generation of suddenly hormone-laden male horndogs came upon the joys and wonders of sexual enlightenment so easily, thanks mostly to the internet. When I was young and searching — and by God, I mean searching — for but the quickest peek at the slip of a female nipple, my son's generation had only to make a few quick strokes on our computer to get around the Parental Controls, then type any sort of smut-laden phrase into the search engine, and there would be nipple slips and a whole lot more right before their eyes in HD and living color. I have to believe that such easy access to these sacred, naughty things made those things seem a whole lot less sacred and naughty to the lucky witness. Maybe that's a good thing, or maybe not; only time will tell.

But I can tell you that having my breath sucked from my lungs, as I was waiting on a young female customer at the Thom McAn shoe store where I was employed, while watching her bend over to fasten the sandal strap on the shoe she was trying on, and her partly open blouse fully revealing her small, braless-breasts, nipple and all, gave me a memory as sacred and naughty as any that I will ever have the pleasure of recalling. Although the vision lasted for only a few short minutes, it sure beat looking at *National Geographic*!

Growing Up at the Mall
IN THE OP

On a brutally hot August 3rd in Overland Park, in the year of 1967, my mother took me, eleven years old, and my five-year-old sister and six-year-old brother, to the grand opening of Metcalf South Shopping Center. Metcalf South was located barely two miles west of our house, and it was at the time of its opening the newest, grandest, and fanciest of indoor shopping malls in the Kansas City area. I honestly can't remember if I was excited or annoyed about attending this event, but I do remember forgetting about every other thing in the world as we stood five rows back from the platform where the ribbon-cutting ceremony occurred, and watching in jaw-dropping awe as the most beautiful human being I ever could have imagined took those large ceremonial scissors and snipped that red ribbon into two. Her name was Deborah Bryant, and she grew up and lived less than a mile south of our house, and she was Miss America. Literally, she *was* Miss America, crowned as such in 1966. I'd never imagined absolute perfection could be wrought so dreamily into the form of a human face. The August heat and humidity, the pomp and circumstance of the mall opening, and the sweaty, noisy, bustling crowd all vanished from the face of my earth as this unimaginable vision of indescribable beauty stood just fifteen feet in front of me. On that day of seeing Deborah Bryant, and walking into the new mall with its endless parade of stores and an atrium with fountains that rose out of sight into the indoor stratosphere, I felt as if I was newly born into a new world, and from that point forward, I was raised and grew up at Metcalf South Shopping Mall.

Growing up in the suburbs of Johnson County didn't afford kids an opportunity to do much with their empty summer days other than play Wiffle ball in the backyard, ride bikes to nowhere in particular, play army/hide & seek in an endless number of homes as they were being built, or, as was the case with me and my immediate talent pool of juvenile delinquents, play with matches and set fields on fire. Sitting inside watching TV absolutely wasn't an option, as we were pretty much booted out the door shortly after sunrise and allowed inside only to eat lunch and pee. However, we mostly peed outside. When Metcalf South opened its doors, here was a new place to while away our hot summer days, inside, in air-conditioned comfort, hanging out without a purpose, and mainly making life hell for the employees of the stores who knew we were doing nothing beyond hanging out without a purpose.

Prior to the opening of Metcalf South, the only other place within walking distance that allowed us the opportunity to sit in air-conditioning was The Drumstick Restaurant, located just south of 95th Street on Nall Avenue. The building still exists today as a liquor store, which it has been for the forty-plus years since The Drumstick closed, save for a very short period when it was a barbecue restaurant. I'm certain that The Drumstick waitstaff's shoddy treatment of us and total disdain for our hard-earned coin played an integral part in the demise of the restaurant. Rarely did a summer day go by that T. Gray and I didn't spend a good hour or two sitting in The Drumstick drinking endless refills of free water, after having spent 10¢ apiece on orders of toasted French Honey Rolls. This culinary delicacy consisted of two egg rolls that had been sliced open and toasted, which we would then slather with copious amounts of free butter and honey, and wash down with free water. Occasionally we would spring for a Coke, served in a glass with chipped ice; the small drink was 15¢, and the large was a quarter, and there were no free refills on the Coke, just the water. It was a real splurge to get the large Coke and an order of toasted French Honey Rolls, the final bill coming in at a hefty 36¢ with tax. And then, feeling as if we were John D. Rockefeller, we'd give the waitress 40¢ and tell her, "Keep the change, baby!" As rare as was the large Coke order, rarer still was the order for actual food — crispy, crunchy fried chicken that they made and sold and from which they attempted to earn their living.

On one of these go-ahead-and-splurge-for-the-large-Coke lazy afternoons in The Drumstick, while wasting away a few idle hours in air-conditioned comfort, I was absentmindedly pouring my free water from the small free-water glass into the now empty, taller large-Coke glass, which I'd drained an hour before. Back and forth, back and forth, until after about the twentieth time of back and forth my dim bulb of a teenage brain finally caught on to the fact that the free-water glass (also happening to be the small-Coke glass) held the exact same volume as the large-Coke glass.

"Hey, wait a minute!" I yelled in the mostly empty restaurant. The waitress perked up and sauntered over to check out the ruckus I had made. When I showed her my little discovery, she smiled, shrugged her shoulders, and walked back to the servers' station, probably hoping — maybe even praying — that my outrage over learning that I was being ripped off whenever I popped the extra dime for a large Coke would have me storming out of the restaurant, vowing never to return. Her prayers would not be answered, as I just took delight in knowing that future visits would net me a large Coke for the price of a small.

Our all-to-frequent annoyances of The Drumstick staff came crashing down one afternoon. Not a lazy summer afternoon, but some months later, probably in January. It was a humdinger of a blizzard that had us out of school and the city virtually shut down. Over two feet of snow had fallen, a heavy, wet snow through which it was almost impossible to walk, but not totally impossible as T. Gray and I braved all for an afternoon trip to The Drumstick. We'd called ahead and, by golly, we hit pay dirt, as even in this weather, they were open. We slogged through the snow, frozen and damp, until we made our way to our slackers' nirvana. *Boy were those toasted French Honey Rolls going to taste good today!* In we walked into the empty restaurant, stamping the snow off our boots and pants as we started to remove our scarves, stocking caps, and coats.

Flo, the headwaitress, had had it with us. "No you don't! Not today, fellas. In fact, not ever again. We don't need your business anymore, so leave, and don't ever come back." From the look on her face, we knew she wasn't kidding. We were dumbfounded, speechless. They were banishing their best, most loyal customers from the restaurant. Why, who else but the most loyal of customers would trudge through two feet of snow to patronize The Drumstick? Us, that's who, with cash in pocket, ready to drop 36¢ for an order of toasted French Honey Rolls and a small Coke; and don't forget the 12-percent tip. The place closed not long after, and both T. Gray and I felt vindicated; it was Karma, before we even knew what Karma was.

✳ ✳ ✳

I was a relatively good kid, not a juvenile delinquent, not a scurvy little hoodlum. There were lots of little hoodlums that hung out at the malls: smoking cigarettes, shoplifting, picking on and getting in fights with other young hoodlums. I referred to them generically as "public school kids," as none of the kids I knew that went to private Catholic schools behaved in that sort of manner. Oh, there were a few troublemakers at Curé of Ars, who I now assume must have had sadomasochistic tendencies, as I've detailed previously that the consequence of malfeasant behavior in a Catholic, nun-laden school was most often physical abuse. You screw up mildly, you'll get your knuckles rapped with a wooden pointer. You screw up big time, and you're looking at that pointer whapping you in the back of the neck so hard that the resultant welt would still be visible into your high school years.

Most pagans who didn't attend Catholic schools thought that nuns used rulers to whap kids. Not the case. I'm certain that sometime in the early 1950s, some industrious nun somewhere came up with the idea of employing the blackboard pointer — a three-foot-long, half-inch-round piece of fire-hardened hickory with a pointed rubber tip on the end. Nuns used them to point at things — numbers, words, sentences — on the blackboard for the purpose of making their point. But the higher purpose of the pointer was as a tool for administering discipline; the "pointing out important stuff" thing was secondary. The pointer was way more aerodynamic than a ruler, as that flatness of a ruler created air drag as it was coming in for a *WHAP!* The smooth, round thinness of the pointer traversed itself through the air at roughly three times the velocity of the standard yardstick ruler, when using an equal degree of swing force. I'm betting the nun that invented using the pointer as a weapon tested, confirmed, and promoted the superior increased velocity of the pointer to the other nuns at their summer nun meetings. And then there was the additional feature of the rubber tip; yes, Sister Vivian could indeed poke and jab at the misbehaving little heathens without worrying about impaling them and drawing blood, much as she would have liked to!

So, the combination of a strict father and a fear of nuns had me pretty much playing life by the rules as a youngster. I only shoplifted once in my life, at the age of sixteen — for whatever reason I now can't imagine — and I got caught. No vandalism, no fistfights, no glue sniffing, no bullying little kids or cruelty to animals. I did have the issue with fire, but, hell, every male kid I knew had an issue with fire.

Possibly the worst thing we did as kids, at the mall, really wasn't all that bad; in fact, I viewed it as an exercise in doing my civic duty — righting a wrong, if you will. I can't remember whether it was T. Gray or I who came up with the clever idea — it was clever enough that I am now happy to take credit for it — of peeing into a plastic grocery produce bag and tying it onto the car door handle on the driver's side. The unsuspecting victims would be walking through the parking lot towards their car, probably whistling a cheerful little tune, anxious to get home with their new purchase, until they happened upon their car. They'd stop dead in their tracks, staring at a plastic bag full of yellow mystery liquid, affixed to their driver's door handle, lying gently against the side of their car door. It would have been summer, and the fluid would have been warm. "What the hell is this?" they'd ask. "And how in the hell am I going to open my car door without dealing with it?" Because, in order for them to get into their car, they had to deal with it. I suppose the other option would have been to climb in on the passenger side, but then they'd be driving down the road with a bag full of urine tied to their door handle, and still yet again, someone would need to deal with it.

Here is where the civic duty part comes in. We didn't randomly select cars for this obscene little gag. We specifically selected cars that were obnoxiously and notably poorly parked — someone who'd purposefully taken up two spaces to avoid people in the next car dinging them when carelessly opening their car door, or someone who'd made their very own space up front, parking beyond the striped outlines and half-parked into the lane of traffic. It was entirely our call as to what was or wasn't an acceptable parking job, but for the most part we were fair and balanced — you park like a selfish pig, you get rewarded with a bag of urine.

In retrospect, I have deep regrets about never staying around to watch the reaction of the bad-parking, urine-bag-winning driver. To see the quizzical then shocked face of some snooty Mercedes driver — more often than not the type of person who felt entitled to more than their fair share of a parking space — would have been satisfying on a level unimaginable. It has also occurred to me that some of these parking lot paybacks could have been misdirected towards an innocent, selfless elderly person who was just a bad parker, a club of which I am now a member.

When Metcalf South opened, it had as its flagship stores a Sears & Roebuck on the south end, and The Jones Store on the north end. In between, there was a Woolworth's drugstore (having a counter with revolving circular stools where you could order malts from an actual soda fountain and paper-thin hamburgers from a flat griddle), a Safeway supermarket (the unwitting participant in our car-door urine gag), a Burstein-Applebee stereo and record store, a Swiss Colony specialty foods store (free samples!), an Orange Julius, Jack Henry men's store, and Gateway Sporting Goods, to name but a few. All of these stores or chains are long gone, with the exceptions of Safeway and Sears, the latter limping along all but barely. Also interspersed amongst the aforementioned stores were a number of clothing and shoe stores, and of paramount importance to this story are the shoe stores. Shoe stores; they hardly even exist any longer, at least not in the fashion or degree to which they existed in the 1970s. Now you buy your shoes at a large box store, with aisle after aisle of boxes of shoes, which you find on your own, measure yourself, try on by yourself, and then trudge up to a line and wait to check out. The shoe stores of yesteryear featured real salespeople who would greet you, measure your foot, then bring out three or four different styles from a hidden and somewhat foreboding backroom. The salesperson would try and sell you shoes, maybe even a second pair of shoes, and more than likely bring over a matching purse or handbag if you were a lady buying ladies' shoes. At the checkout register, the salesperson would offer you socks, pantyhose, shoe polish, or waterproofing spray for your winter boots. At the core of this was customer service; excellent customer service made the customer happy and the store money. This concept of customer service, like the stand-alone shoe store, is sadly becoming a thing of the past.

In Metcalf South, there were five stand-alone shoe stores: Bakers, shoes for women; Steve's Shoes and Robinson's Shoes, higher-end stores that sold name brands like Nunn Bush and Florsheim; and Thom McAn and Kinney's, lower-priced, full-line shoes stores, i.e., men's, women's, and children's shoes. Chances were if you shopped at Thom McAn and Kinney's, you didn't shop at Steve's or Robinson's, which were notably more expensive as they carried shoes that were purportedly of higher quality. The reverse was mostly true; my father wouldn't buy shoes at Thom McAn or Kinney's because he thought they were cheaply made with poor quality materials. Soles were glued to the "upper," rather than stitched; most often the soles weren't leather, but plastic, as was often the lining as well. Even after I began working at Thom McAn, he refused to buy or wear Thom McAn shoes. When he was a young boy in Hannibal, Missouri, my father's first paying job was at the International Shoe Company factory, located south of downtown Hannibal in the small industrial district. It was the largest employer in Hannibal at the time, providing the US military with shoes and boots, as well as a full line of shoes for the rest of America. They made shoes of high quality, with real leather uppers and liners, and leather soles that were hand stitched to the uppers. Due to his hands-on experience of making the shoes, my father knew what a good shoe was, and not in hell would he go against his hard-earned, ingrained standards and wear a pair of cheap, crappy Thom McAn shoes. Johnny Carson had a running gag that made fun of Thom McAn shoes, which I'm sure the executives at the Ward Melville Shoe Company of Rye, New York, both loved and hated. (Melville Shoe was the parent company of Thom McAn.)

They no longer make high quality shoes in Hannibal, Missouri (nor anywhere else in the United States); Thom McAn Shoes no longer exists; Melville Corporation is now CVS; Johnny Carson is sadly long departed and late-night TV no longer makes jokes about anything as mundane and harmless as shoe stores. Progress? I think not.

Leap ahead from my bike-riding, urine-bag-tying aimless summers as a fourteen-year-old, to the summer of 1972, which was the summer of my sixteenth birthday. A sixteenth birthday is one of life's most significant, as youngsters are now legally able to do two things that they'll do for most of the rest of their lives; two things that will bless them, provide for them, possibly define them, bring them joy, bring them pain, and very possibly kill them — driving and working. On the day of my sixteenth birthday, I mined a dry hole in my first attempt to procure my driver's license. I easily passed the written part of the test but had a little issue on the driving part when I came within a few feet of mowing down a hitchhiker. The guy was much quicker than he looked, and that was a good thing for him, as he dove away from the road as I passed by, me not giving one inch as I drove razor straight in my lane, the lane that I presumed was my right-of-way. As the hitchhiker leapt away from the street, the State Trooper giving me the test squawked, and loudly barked "You almost hit that guy! Why didn't you pull over?" I was a little dumbfounded by the question. Everyone knows that hitchhiking is illegal. Not only has he no right to stand by the side of a busy road with his thumb in the air, it is in fact against the law for him to do so. That was my firm answer, and I was firmly told I would not be getting my license on my sixteenth birthday, but would have to wait a week before I came back for a second go at it. I was counseled that no matter what a person may or may not be doing in or near the street, the prudent course would be to avoid smacking into them. My second try at the test wrought no hitchhikers or other moral dilemmas to ponder as I navigated the tree-lined streets of Johnson County, and I did in fact gain my driver's license.

Concurrent with the driver's license came the first job. It would be a job that I'd have until I got out of college, and a year beyond as I actually worked there full-time and thought about making a career out of Melville Shoe Corporation. I still have dreams (mostly nightmares) about having multiple customers in the kids' section: children are wailing, climbing all over me; mothers are cranky; we're out of every size that I need; and it's the Saturday before Easter. I know that scenario doesn't sound quite like the fire and fury of a charge up Pork Chop Hill, but let me tell you, minus the threat of death, a busy Saturday in the kids' section at Thom McAn was on a trauma level pretty close to the flying bullets and bloodcurdling screams present during the heat of armed conflict. I'm not kidding.

As a new hire at Thom McAn, you were immediately relegated to the kids' section, which was located in the back of the store where all of the children's shoes were displayed, fitted, and sold. The area was roughly two hundred square feet, with the shoes displayed on two separate tiers of racks that were affixed to the back wall. There were six chairs lined up perpendicular to each of the display racks, and in the center of the area was a small, circular display table with seasonal shoes — sneakers and sandals in the summer, boots and galoshes in the winter. Children's shoes were the toughest to sell, and were priced for far less than the women's and men's shoes. Thus, the more experienced sales people got the benefit of easier, costlier sales, and the higher commissions that came along with them. Commission rates for women's and men's shoes were 1.5 percent; children's shoes paid 2 percent; purses, socks, and accessories paid 5 percent; and shoe polish and cleaners, shoelaces and shoe trees paid 10 percent.

"Wait a minute!" you're saying. "Children's shoes paid 2 percent commission, which is more than the 1.5 percent women's and men's shoes paid." The average kid's shoe cost $7.99, which netted the sales clerk a hefty 16¢ in commission, while the average adult shoe cost $20.00, which paid a whopping 30¢. And, it took about twice as long to sell a pair of kid's shoes as compared to selling shoes to an adult. Financially, it was loserville if you were stuck back in the kids' section. Unfortunately, my inherently kind and patient nature made me a success at selling children's shoes, and I ended up spending the better part of my career stuck back in the kids' section on busy, potentially-profitable-for-most-of-the-other-sales-people Saturdays. It wouldn't be the first time in my life, nor would it be the last, that my good nature would get me in trouble.

I was in the kids' section on busy weekend days, but I was free to roam the store and sell the whole shebang on weeknights, which I generally worked two or three times a week. It was very early in my tenure, maybe my third week at Thom McAn, that I was working on a slow Wednesday night in August. I was waiting on a young lady, who I would guess was maybe twenty years of age, and she was interested in a pair of sandals. She was very pretty, and very friendly; not flirty or anything like that, just friendly. She picked her sandal from the display, and I went in the back room, retrieved the shoes, and brought them back out to her. I opened the box, took out the right sandal, and began to get down on one knee to put it on her foot. This is what shoe salespeople did back then — they actually put the shoe on the customer's foot. As I began to kneel, the young lady quickly waved me off, took the sandal, and said that she'd put it on herself. No problem, I thought, and handed her the shoe. As she bent over to fasten the sandal strap, her low-cut, white-linen peasant blouse gaped open, fully exposing her small, unrestrained, braless breasts, nipples and all. It took her a minute to fasten the buckle, and I stood staring down her shirt, my mouth agape, yet I was unable to draw a breath. Anyone watching me from afar might have thought I was on the verge of having an epileptic seizure. These were the first, real-live breasts that I had ever seen, and at the time, it was the most gloriously beautiful sight that I had ever witnessed. She finally sat upright, and asked me for the other sandal. My God, I was going to get to see them again! And again, she bent over and displayed to me a little piece of heaven in the flesh. She got up from the chair and walked a few steps to the mirror to see how the sandals looked on her feet, came back, sat down, and repeated the whole process all over again as she took the shoes off. "I don't think so," she said, "but thank you for your help." I didn't say a word. Not a "Can I show you another style?" or "Thank you for stopping in!" I said nothing, because I was too flummoxed to speak. I do remember thinking, as I stood there with an unsold box of sandals in my hands, watching the most beautiful thing that I'd ever seen walk out of my life, that I was pretty sure I was going to enjoy selling shoes.

Along with my first job came my first boss. And, oh, what a first boss he was! His name was Bill Haupt, a six-foot-two, rail-thin ex-Army drill instructor from Dallas, Texas. He had thick, wavy brown hair in kind of a puffed-up bouffant, and sideburns that almost went into a lambchop.

(Picture Elvis, or Chris Issak.) This was 1972, and hair was longer, clothes were hideously horrific, and big, bushy, long sideburns were in vogue. Looking at pictures from that time makes you wonder what in God's name we were thinking.

I was a small, skinny, pimply-faced kid with thick, longish, wavy hair with all sorts of dips and curls. Again, I look at pictures of myself and shudder. I was the one of us siblings who had the bad fortune to have their high school senior-class portrait taken when that hairstyle was fashionable, and it hung on the wall of my parents' hallway into my later years, a lasting memorial to the awkwardness of the 1970s adolescent male. When you add oversized, cuffed bell-bottom pants, screamingly loud floral or paisley silk or nylon shirts, and platform shoes to the mix, you have a look that would make clown-car occupants green with envy. For a fact, this skinny-assed clown-car occupant had no clue as to what he was in for in the person of US Army Sergeant William T. Haupt, now retired from the service but still very much in midcareer military form.

Every Saturday at 9:00 a.m. sharp, you were required to be at the Thom McAn store, sitting in the chairs back in my beloved kids' section for a nonpaid sales meeting — an hour-long, weekly masterpiece performance of selling tips, motivational pep talks, old war stories, violent outbursts, and general amped-up, high-volume, verbal hysteria. It was a thing of sheer dramatic beauty, wrapped up in a blanket of fear and intimidation. Nothing anyone ever did was good enough. No matter how many pairs of shoes we sold that prior week, how many sales records we continued to break, or how many budgets we exceeded, it was never good enough.

An example: "Worsfeld, what the hell kind of shit day did you have last Saturday? I gave you exclusive control of the men's section, and you barely farted out $700 worth of shoes. I could book seven-hundred bucks before lunch on a bad day in men's, hungover with a broken thumb. I want a thousand out of you today, or next Saturday you're gonna find your ass back in the kids' section with Pimple-faced Paradise!"

All of this he would yell, at the top of his lungs, as if we were in fact getting ready to charge up Pork Chop Hill and, by God, the lives and well-being of every red-blooded American man, women, and child depended upon our success. Good grief; we were teenagers, with a part-time job selling shoes! And, as I said, we weren't even getting paid to sit through these Saturday morning beatdowns.

One of his classics went something like this. After a forty-minute dress down of every one of his employees, first as a group and then individually, the senior salesman, A. J. Worsfeld, got the gumption (or had the bad sense) to question the mighty Haupt.

"But Bill," Worsfeld began, timidly, "I don't think we're doing that bad. We're ahead of our budget this month, and we're way ahead of our year-to-date budget. I actually think we're doing a pretty good job."

Silence for a few seconds. Haupt looked up at the ceiling, his eyes closed, and then took both of his hands and started rubbing his face, as if he were trying to wipe away the tension that was building up like a steam boiler. He then crossed his arms and, with his right hand, pinched the bridge of his nose, his eyes still closed. Now acting composed, he began, quietly. "You think you're doing a pretty good job?" Then a little louder. "You think you're doing a pretty good job? Well let me tell you something." And then, the explosion. "Robinson's, across the mall from us ... their doors are still open! Steve's Shoes, right over there (he pointed out the door in the direction of Steve's), their doors are still open! Baker's doors are open! Kinney's doors are open. When every one of them have shut their doors and gone out of business, then you can dare to open your fat mouth and tell me you think you're doing a pretty good job!"

Had he a mic, this would have been the moment to drop it. Instead, he slowly looked around at each of the assembled employees, one by one, to see if anyone would dare utter a peep in defiance, until he finally came to T. Gray, who sat quietly with a shoe in one hand and a shoe brush in the other.

"Just what in the hell do you think you're doing?"

"Uh ... shining my shoes, Bill."

"Shining your shoes! Shining your shoes! Goddammit, this is MY sales meeting, and this is MY time, and I'll be goddamned if I'm going to pay you to sit there and shine your shoes during my time. Shine your goddamn shoes on your own time! Got it?"

Haupt then stormed back into his office, leaving the unpaid and slightly bemused staff to contemplate his masterful performance. Were it committed to celluloid, it would have garnered a hundred years' worth of Oscars. By God, it was brilliant.

It wasn't long after that I was personally on the receiving end of another of Bill's Masterpiece Theater-worthy ass chewing's. It was a weeknight, and I do not recall the particulars of what set him off. It could have been a few lackluster weeks of sales performance on my part, and probably on the part of the whole sales team. Haupt left the store about 7:00 to head to Pappy's BBQ, located in the lower level of the mall. It wasn't unusual on a slow night for him to go down there, as he liked to drink beer, and there was a waitress who worked there with whom I believe he was extracurricularing. He came back to the store at our 9:00 closing time, and more than likely he was on the verge of inebriation; this was never a good thing with Haupt. Again, I don't remember the exact thing that set him off, but I very quickly found myself in the back aisle, rigid and up against a wall full of shoeboxes, with Bill Haupt nose to nose with me, much like the interchanges you might remember seeing with Sergeant Carter and Gomer Pyle.

He began at the top of his lungs. "YOU … THINK … YOU'RE … COOL? … YOU … THINK … YOU'RE … COOL? … I'M … ASKING … YOU … A … QUESTION! … YOU … THINK … YOU'RE … COOL?"

I was absolutely petrified, and I had no idea where he was going with this.

"Uh … no," I leaked out.

"WELL I THINK YOU THINK YOU'RE COOL. YOU BEBOPPIN' AROUND HERE IN YOUR BELL-BOTTOM PANTS AND YOUR PLATFORM SHOES LIKE SOME SORT OF FIVE-DOLLAR PIMP. WHAT, YOU THINK YOU'RE DOWN ON 12TH STREET, WALKING UP AND DOWN PIMPING WHORES? WELL DO YOU? YOU USED TO BE PIMPLE FACE, BUT NOW YOU'RE PIMP. PARADISE THE PIMP. YOU LIKE THAT? YOU THINK THAT'S COOL?"

"Uh … no." Was all I could muster.

The yelling stopped, as did the anger, but we were still nose to nose and eyeball to eyeball. "Lemme tell you somethin'… Pimp. You got one week to turn things around and show me you got what it takes to stay in my army. You got that? I want you here, but I want you to get your shit together. So get it together. You gonna get it together?"

"Yes, sir."

"You want to be here?"

"Yes, sir."

"Good. Now get your ass out there and vacuum that sales floor." And off he went.

I was a sixteen-year-old kid, making $1.60 an hour, selling shoes at the mall. I could have walked out and found a hundred other part-time jobs that didn't involve working for a drunken ex-drill sergeant. But I didn't. I stayed, I got my shit together, and I worked in that shoe store, off and on, for the next seven years. I never told my parents about this, because I wasn't entirely sure what they would do — make me quit, confront Haupt, yell at me for being a slacker? I figured that I was old enough to drive, old enough to work, and old enough to suffer the consequences of poor performance. I was also old enough to learn that the bubble of love within which we are raised can quickly be burst when you venture out into the world. The sooner one comes to grips with that fact, the better the chances of survival. Bill Haupt shattered my bubble, for which I am eternally grateful, and I would thank him for that today if I were lucky enough to have the opportunity.

Literally and figuratively, I really did grow up at Metcalf South Shopping Center. From the ages of eleven through sixteen, the mall was my summer playground. From my sixteenth birthday through my college years, it was my employer. It provided me with everything that I wore and a large percentage of what I ate and drank. Metcalf South housed The Record Bar, the store I visited on an almost daily basis to talk music with the cool older guys that worked there, educating and fostering in me the healthiest of addictions that still cripples me today — my love of music.

Just a few doors down from the Record Bar was the arcade, where I spent most of my hours that weren't spent working at the shoe store. Before work, on my lunch break, or after work, I was diligently, 25¢ at a time, practicing for my ultimate career as a professional pinball player. I really thought I was that good, working pinball magic in front of my friends, who were ensorcelled by the silver flashes that rocketed off my flippers, deftly nailing target after target. I actually believed I was good enough to compete on a national stage in high-dollar pinball championships against the other slacker punks who spent the better part of their lives in a mall arcade, hunched over a Mata Hari or Tommy pinball machine. Sad that the University of Kansas didn't offer a degree in pinball.

Metcalf South was where I smoked my first cigarette, as the mall housed a cigarette machine in the Woolworth's where, uncarded, I bought Camel Filters for 50¢ a pack. The mall also employed the first girl I ever seriously kissed, she the vixen who was also responsible for selling me on the positive attributes of tobacco addiction; as you more than likely guessed, these two events were inextricably linked. Had you told me the day before

I smoked my first cigarette that in just a few short days I would willingly be dropping quarters into a machine to buy a product that would make my teeth yellow, foul my breath, stink up my car and clothes, and put a quick end to my soccer career, I'd have told you that you needed to have your head examined. The girl was out of my life in less than a month; unfortunately, the cigarettes stayed with me for six long years.

The first girl that I ever loved worked at the mall, as did the second. Both of them worked at Topsy's on the middle level, just a few doors down from Thom McAn. I was pretty convinced that I would marry and spend the rest of my life with my first love. When that went suddenly and unexpectedly south, I thought my world had come to an end. And it did for a short while, until I fell hard for the next girl that worked at Topsy's. You all know the drill. Love can be a lot like beer, in that the one that you have in your hand at the time is the best one you've ever had, and the only one you'll ever need, until you finish with it, and you quickly find yourself searching for another.

I met my wife at the mall. On a summer evening after graduating from college, while filling in for someone at Thom McAn who'd begged me to cover a shift, I noticed a beautiful young woman who was sitting in the store, not to buy shoes, but waiting for her friend who happened to be one of my coworkers. I couldn't help but feel that she was checking me out as I waited on customers, so of course I started showing off a bit, the way professional shoe dogs often will — flipping shoes in the air and catching them behind your back before putting them on the customer's foot, loudly and with a dramatic flair guessing shoe sizes of customers without using the Brannock Device for measuring, leaping to pull a box of shoes out of the high wall, shunning the aid of a step stool. Simply put, I executed a lot of cool stunts that would impress any young, beautiful, impressionable woman. In spite of my painfully nerdish behavior that evening, we went on to date and marry, and these many years later, I'm still trying every day to impress her.

Speaking of many years later, in 2017 they tore down Metcalf South. I watched in slow-motion horror (as did most of my OP contemporaries) over the course of a few months as the bulldozers and excavators, bite by painful bite, tore away at that massive structure where I played, where I worked, where I all but lived, but most importantly, where I grew up and lost my youthful innocence, and after doing so, found the rest of my life. It was the saddest of sights that I would never have imagined. This was the most brutal of reminders that nothing lasts forever, except for your beautiful memories.

Growing Up Lucky IN THE OP

Improving upon a famous quote by Branch Rickey, a former boss of mine used to say, "Luck is the residue of good design." In my case, for the most part I don't agree with that adage, as most of my life's successes have been one piece of blind good luck stacked on top of another, with no evidence of even a shred of good design. Also, you can simply look at many of the OP stories I've detailed in this book and know for a fact that most of the predicaments I've been lucky enough to survive came about because of very bad design. There is no question that had certain things gone just slightly one way or another, I would not have lived to pen these stories. I can also say that on a few rare occasions, if not for luck, had certain things gone one way or the other, I might be penning these stories from the Kansas State Penitentiary, located up the road a bit from the OP, in Lansing, Kansas.

From as early as I can remember, I loved music. More than likely this came from growing up in a house where every evening, prior to sitting down at the table for our family dinner, my father would come home from work, notably exhausted, sit in the living room with a "highball" in hand, and read the evening newspaper while listening to his record player. A couple of important points of explanation are in order to those who are not my contemporaries. First off, I have no earthly idea where the term "highball" came from when referencing a cocktail; it was all I knew them as when growing up, but the term disappeared, never to reappear, as I hit my college years and started pounding down highballs on my own. My father's highball of choice was scotch and water, and I don't ever recall him or my mother drinking them to excess. For Dad, it was the one or two before dinner, and for my mother, it was the occasional Manhattan on the weekend. I do remember that my parents had a Berbiglia charge account (*the* local KC-area liquor store chain), so possibly there was a lot more hooch consumption happening than I was aware of, but their lives and subsequent successes showed no signs of it.

A second point of explanation goes to my father reading the evening newspaper. That paper would have been the *Kansas City Star*, and it would have been the second newspaper he would have read on any particular day, as he'd have already read the morning newspaper, the *Kansas City Times*, with his breakfast and coffee. That evening newspaper would disappear in 1990, when the paper's owners decided to scrap it and just offer up one daily newspaper, in the morning, and adopt the *Kansas City Star* name for that paper. As with many major city newspapers these days, the *Kansas City Star* is hardly but a shell of what it once was — blame the internet and cable news channels, or, dare I say, blame the owners for not delivering a product that the masses find worth the exorbitant prices that the *Star* commands. When I walk my three-mile exercise trek through my neighborhood every morning, I generally pick up the newspaper from the gutters and dew-laden yards where it is often chucked by the less-than-attentive carrier, and lay it up near the front porches of the respective homes, saving the owners a few steps, steps that can better be spent later in the day. I am amazed at the limited number of houses that still receive the newspaper, easily in the maximum range of 10 percent. When I was young, every house got the paper, thus it is easy to see why the *KC Star* is now nearing the brink of being unable to sustain itself. Is this progress, or is it an example of the residue of bad design?

The final point of explanation involves the record player. When we lived in our first house on Somerset, the record player was a large, rectangular piece of furniture, roughly the size of a washing machine. It was constructed of high-quality wood, with a single large speaker in the front, which was obscured by cloth mesh and some decorative wicker. The unit opened from the top, much like the washing machine, and there sat the simple turntable, with a spindle and an automatic arm that would magically lift, retract, and gently ensconce itself in its cradle after the LP had run its course; this unprovoked motion certainly seemed magical to a four-year-old. One of the first absolutes that I learned as a four-year-old was never in hell was I to touch that magical record player, which was referred to as the "hi-fi," short for high fidelity.

Shortly after we moved to our larger home on Briar, my father acquired a "stereo," which was indeed a beautiful wooden piece of furniture, roughly the height and length of a credenza, and the focal point of our living room. It contained the same magical turntable underneath its sliding door, which was located on the top of the unit, but this hi-fi had two speakers, not one, and it played records that were specially recorded to take advantage of two speakers. I remember going to the SupeRx drugstore at 95th and Nall, next door to the Kroger store, and always on the agenda was thumbing through the small section of record albums, never for the purpose of buying them, but just to keep tabs on what was there. Occasionally I'd go with my older brother, Ron, he being the owner of a simple record player, and watch as he'd have an internal debate with himself about popping the extra dollar for a record that was recorded in stereo, versus the cheaper version that was simply recorded in hi-fi. Even though his record player had only one speaker, there was a thought that the sound of the stereo version was superior to the hi-fi recording. Also, in the one-in-a-million chance that our father would play that record on his stereo, well then, we were covered. Make that one-in-ten-million, as Dad was possessive of his stereo to the point of it being a neurosis. For this guy who grew up during the Great Depression with nothing, this beautiful extravagance, this ultimate symbol of high-tech mad money, was his and his alone. Not ever, under any imaginable circumstance, were we allowed to lay a finger on his stereo; if you even got close enough to breathe on it, he'd shudder and shake, barking at you to back off.

It wasn't long after the acquisition of this monument to success that the game for my older brother and sister was to play their records on the stereo when my parents were gone. And a game it was, as my father had an acute sense of when things weren't just the way he left them. Off my parents would drive for a Saturday evening of friends, highballs, and Manhattans, and my siblings would make a beeline for the stereo. It would be carefully examined before it was touched: had Dad left the top door open one inch or two; was the volume knob turned between three and four, or was it between four and five? It had better be exactly the way Dad left it, or there would be hell to pay. The thought of something as raw and radical as the Beatles blasting out of his precious stereo speakers, fouling them, all but desecrating them, was simply more than AJP could bear. Even though both my brother and sister had small record players in their rooms, upon which they could play their

45s, and the occasional album that they'd sacrificed a few weeks allowance to procure, the tinny, muted sound that came from those small two-inch speakers was akin to being projected from the bottom of an empty beer can when compared to the full-blown, stereophonic music that emanated from my father's stereo speakers, especially when we'd jack those speakers beyond the five spot on the volume knob, which produced a veritable chorus of seraphim trumpets, raining down upon us from above.

Back to the music. On my father's tightly regulated stereo playlist, I grew up listening to the stalwarts of my father's era: The Glenn Miller Orchestra, Stan Getz, Frank Sinatra, Nat King Cole, Peggy Lee, and the like. I remember lying on the living room floor with my father and my two older siblings, with the lights turned off, listening to a slow build to the fabulous crescendo of Ravel's *Boléro*, all of us oblivious to the sexual undertones of the piece; my father said it reminded him of an ever-growing-larger parade of camels as they trundled over the desert sands. I remember listening to Andy Williams sing "Moon River," a song and singer that typically brought my mother into the room, dirty dishes waiting in the sink to be dealt with be damned. The ultimate highlight of our lives for a few months involved listening over and over again to the Spike Jones & His City Slickers greatest hits album, a level of musical parody, comic timing, and cornball cleverness that has never since been matched. I haven't heard it for a while, but I bet it would still make me laugh.

As I was wired into an appreciation of music from the get-go, it made the arrival of the Beatles a little like putting rocket fuel into a Ferrari for the first time. They were arguably the most dynamic cultural event the world had ever witnessed, before or since. My music-loving father hated their music, he hated their hair, and, most importantly, like so many of his generation, he hated the omnipresent effect that they had upon his children. Like most of my baby-boomer contemporaries, I'll never forget the Beatles first appearance on *The Ed Sullivan Show*, my whole family parked in front of our small black-and-white television. My older sister was that girl who shrieked and held the sides of her head as if she were in such a profound state of ecstasy that it was torturous, while my brother and I were simply transfixed, as they were the absolutely coolest humans we had ever seen. Every move of their heads, every tap of their boots, every smile of joy that came from *their* realization that they were the real deal made them seem to us more akin to gods than mortals. Throughout the ordeal, my mother sat quietly, while my father made caustic remarks, fighting for, and losing, the battle for verbal airspace with his enraptured daughter.

I still hear certain Beatles' songs from their early catalogue and wonder how my father couldn't have found something positive in the music. As they grew in popularity, fighting through the "we're more popular than Jesus" issue, and then the longer hair, and the drugs, and the Maharishi phase, these things only reinforced my father's dislike of them. We were prohibited from owning *The White Album*; I had to listen to it at friends' houses, friends who had way cooler parents than I. Now in my 60's, a span of five years seems like yesterday — the groundbreaking cultural shift from 1964 until 1969 that the Beatles brought upon us was a staggering feat. They went from mop-topped kids to the ultimate counterculture rebels, and society's youth and culture rode right along with them. Our generation's music went from the Beatles on *Ed Sullivan* on a small black-and-white television to an epic culture-defining event like Woodstock, in the absolute blink of an eye. Unbelievable!

While many from my generation of fellow OP'ers may claim this, my older sister really did see the Beatles at Municipal Stadium, at that time the home to Charlie Finley's Kansas City Athletics Major League Baseball team, taken by my oldest cousin. Another famous OP concert of note involved The Who playing at Shawnee Mission South High School in 1967, actually opening for The Buckinghams. While the attendance figures are unavailable, roughly 150,000 OP'ers now claimed to have been there. My brother and I were not so lucky. Our first concert of record was at Municipal Auditorium, which was located a few short blocks from the 12th Street string of strip clubs and dive bars, when my father took us, along with one of his good friends and his two sons, to see Herb Alpert & The Tijuana Brass. It was a real coup for both Ron and me that my father associated with, and actually liked, this new, hot group that we liked; he would even on occasion allow my brother to play his Herb Alpert records on his stereo. Good thing my brother dropped the extra buck for the stereo version.

My next concert was also witnessed in the presence of my father, as sometime in 1971 he took T. Gray and I to see Cat Stevens at The Music Hall, which was also in downtown Kansas City, MO, adjacent to the Municipal Auditorium. It was the classic example of two worlds colliding, as my father sucked it up and found himself amongst a crowd of pot-smoking, long-haired hippies, watching a quiet concert in the same staid concert hall where he'd occasionally watch the Kansas City Symphony perform. T. Gray and I quickly wanted to die, as my father would gape open-mouthed, point, and gasp at the long-hairs as if he were a five-year-old being dragged through the freak show at the State Fair. The final bit of torture came when he would jump from his seat and chastise nearby patrons for smoking in this nonsmoking venue — cigarettes or pot, it made no difference. NO SMOKING meant no smoking! Poor Cat Stevens had a bit of a breakdown on stage that evening; it was such a trauma in his life that he later wrote a song about it entitled "18th Avenue (Kansas City Nightmare)." I can't help but believe that my father's bad vibes thundered their way down the aisles and up onto the stage of the Music Hall that evening. It was the last rock concert I attended with my father.

As soon as I was old enough to have friends that drove, I regularly attended concerts, most of which were "lesser" bands that played at Memorial Hall, located at 7th and Barnett in Kansas City, Kansas. The theme of this chapter is luck, and I was lucky enough to grow up in a time when the music of a generation, my generation, was so accessible, weekly, in a venue small enough that my weak arm could hurl a baseball from one side to the next. No matter where you sat, you were immersed in the show, all but on top of the stage, seeing the likes of pre-stadium popularity Led Zeppelin, Jethro Tull, Genesis, Fleetwood Mac, The Grateful Dead, Billy Joel, U2, and on and on and on. I'd go to one concert after the next, few of which my parents knew about ("Gonna be working late at Thom McAn tonight, doing inventory!"), and made a lifetime's worth of musical memories in a few short years. It always amazed me that I'd keep seeing the same people at these concerts, people that I'd never see anywhere in the OP, or anywhere in Johnson County for that matter. I'd wonder: where in the hell do these people live; why are they at every damn concert; and why do I never see them anywhere else other than at these concerts? It never occurred to me that they were probably thinking the same about me.

Like many of my contemporaries, I think contemporary popular music is a few steps below being absolute crap, at best (with a very few exceptions). I fervently believe that the music that shaped my youth, while forever shaping the face of popular music, will be around for centuries to come, not unlike Bach, Beethoven, Mozart, and their ilk. I also believe that most of today's popular music — namely rap, bad female-anthem Lady Gaga- and Taylor Swift-stuff, bald guys wearing big cowboy hats country music, and rap, again — won't even be a footnote in the historical significance of musical trends. Call me an old OP idiot, but check with me in a hundred years, and we'll see who was right!

✳ ✳ ✳

    Nineteen seventy-two was a pretty big year for me. It was the year I turned sixteen; it was the year of my first job; the year that I got my driver's license; and, very shortly after, the year I got my first car. My first car, also my best car and my absolutely worst car, was a 1972 Chevy Vega GT Hatchback, white with a black stripe down the center, nicknamed Moe. Moe was a four-speed, shift-on-the-floor, white-hot rocket, or so it seemed when I finally figured out how to drive its manual transmission.

    However, Moe wasn't even close to being considered a real car until I had saved enough cash to drop it off at the CMC Car Stereo Center, located at 79th Street and Metcalf Avenue, right in the heart of the OP, and have a state-of-the-art, $200, eight-track, four-speaker car stereo system installed. Oh, the joys and wonders of the eight-track tape! The most important component of any eight-track tape player was a book of matches, which you would use eternally to jam between the mouth of the unit and the eight-track tape to stop it from playing two songs at the same time. If you had a new, crisp eight-track tape, and a high-end unit, you might get four or five clean plays before the tape began wobbling and skipping and playing track one at the same time it was playing track four. At this point, you'd need to pull the car over, jam in a new, taut matchbook whilst scrunching your eyes and nose and holding your tongue just right, and you might get that damn tape to play just the one song you wanted to hear, for a few minutes, before it squiggled, wobbled, and ultimately ate the tape right out of the plastic cartridge as it digested your music into the bowels of your $200 CMC-installed tape player. While the quality of the music has degenerated over the past forty years, thankfully, the technology that now delivers shitty contemporary music has, conversely, greatly improved.

    My father helped me buy the Vega from a business associate who worked at the General Motors plant in Kansas City; GM was a major customer of my father's company. I bought the car for $1500: $500 of which I'd saved, $500 that my father gifted me, and $500 that I borrowed from Ranch Mart Bank. According to my father, you were never too young to start building your credit, or, as was the case with me, never too young to start ruining your credit with a slow payment or two. The car was used, but only nine-months-old, having been gently driven from September through May by twin brothers during their senior year in high school, approximately 2300 miles per month, around the city of Independence, MO. That would be enough miles to drive back and forth to your local grocery store about 5,000 times in a 270-day span; or, more dramatically, it would equate to three round trips from New York City to San Francisco, CA, downshifting, breaking, stopping, and starting every few miles. Simply put, these two hellions drove the piss out of that car in a very short amount of time. My new-to-me Vega may have been nine-months-old, but due to its brief but profound history of use and abuse, it had the body of a ninety-year-old. They'd already put a new transmission in the car by the time they sold it to me; I'd see them a new transmission, and raise them one, by the time that car finally gave up the ghost.

The Vega sat parked in the street next to our driveway more often than it cruised the mean streets of the OP, always broken down, always waiting on me to come up with the cash for the needed replacement part in the form of an 18,000-mile-old alternator, or fuel pump, or diverter valve. It should have been a bad omen to me when on the first day I drove the car to Rockhurst High School early in my junior year, as I sat proudly in the parking lot after school, showing the car to my broke-dick classmates who had not the wherewithal to purchase such a fine specimen of mechanized independence, my open drivers-side car door was swiped out of existence by an inattentive classmate passing too closely in his fine specimen of an automobile. From that point forward with that car, it was one piece of bad luck after the next.

I was barely able to will that car to college, driving it slowly to the University of Kansas (KU), hoping to just get it to the fraternity house parking lot. You could walk or take the bus around Lawrence to get to class, and you could always hitch rides back to the OP on the weekend with people who didn't own ninety-year-old Vegas. But the key thing was having a car, and although it rarely started, and barely ran when it did start, I did have a car of my own at the frat house. There were sixty guys in my fraternity, but only twenty possessed cars, which meant that twenty cars were divided amongst sixty nineteen-year-old hell-on-wheels males and their girlfriends, their dogs, and multiple other frat friends and their friends. It might have been a nice, relatively new car that your parents fronted you. But more than likely in the mid-70s, it was a beater Pontiac Bonneville from the late 60s that comfortably sat eight of your frat brothers, which was good, because you'd need all eight of them to help push the thing when it ran out of gas or threw a rod. Or it was my car, and the rule with Moe was: If you can start it, you can borrow it. Just put some gas in it!

Moe's last big run was a night in late October, during my senior year at KU. A group of six fraternity brothers — me not amongst them — borrowed the car to drive it to a pumpkin patch in nearby Eldora, Kansas, on a late-night mission to steal pumpkins for our upcoming Halloween Barn Party, known as the "Oskaloosa Outrage." I believe they chose my car as it would be the least likely of all the frat-house cars to be missed should they have to abandon it in the midst of their nefarious activities. They did return it, but I'm pretty certain they left a large portion of the transmission in that pumpkin patch. Not long after, I attempted to drive the car home to Kansas City late on a Friday night for the purpose of working a Saturday shift at Thom McAn. I crept along the newly opened stretch of K-10 to just a few miles south of Kansas State Highway K-7, when poor old Moe pumped its last piston stroke at about 1:00 a.m. With no cell phone, no pay phone, and no sign of any human being, I began the fifteen-mile walk to 97th and Juniper in the OP. Fortunately I was picked up by another late-night KU-to-OP commuter, but Moe would sit on the side of that highway for a few days before I could get a tow truck to deposit him back in his comfortable street-side parking spot next to my parents' driveway.

Here is the ultimate injustice, all but a desecration of the dead. The car sat there for months. I had no money to get it running, nor the time, interest, or cash to give it a proper burial. One morning when my father was leaving for work, he noticed glass shards in the street next to Moe, and saw that the small window in the back seat had been shattered. Upon closer inspection, he noticed that someone had broken into the car and stolen both the driver and passenger front bucket seats out of the car. I suppose they were the only things of value left to a parts thief, as the CMC eight-track stereo player had long since been made obsolete and worthless at the hands of the latest technology, the no-matchbook-required, single-track cassette player.

Big concert lucky, and big life lucky, happened to me on the evening of June 22nd, 1972. As mentioned earlier, most of the fledgling musical groups that I would pay money to see played at the all-but-intimate 3500-seat Memorial Hall in Kansas City, Kansas, while the big established acts played at the 10,000-seat Municipal Auditorium in downtown Kansas City, and then in the 20,000-seat Kemper Arena, after it opened in 1974. During my sophomore year of high school, I stumbled upon a gig of ushering at Municipal Auditorium. It didn't pay much — I think I got eight bucks a show — but I got into the concerts for free and could actually sit in any open seat during the main act. We'd usher people to their seats during the warm-up act, go pick up our cigarette and Boone's Farm money, and then we were free to enjoy the headliners. At least that was the routine until the evening of June 22nd, 1972. On that night, Municipal Auditorium was home to the Rolling Stones, at that time the Greatest Rock & Roll Band in the World, and the recent creators of still one of the greatest rock & roll albums of all time, *Exile on Main Street*. Not even arguably. Tickets to this show were sold out immediately, and priced way beyond my financial ken. I quickly pulled rank as one of the finest ushers the keepers of Municipal Auditorium had ever known, and was signed up on a very exclusive list to usher at the concert, but there would be no eight-dollar payday. And finding an empty seat to enjoy the main act was going to be the tallest of tall orders. I was able to recruit a friend who went to Rockhurst High School and worked at the grocery store in Prairie Village Shopping Center to usher with me, but more importantly, to drive me, as I was a few months shy of getting my driver's license. The plan was working out well until I found out that my buddy couldn't get his family car that night; he was child number six of eight, and as a newly licensed sixteen-year-old, he was pretty low on the totem pole when it came to borrowing their only family automobile. But as luck would have it, he worked with a guy at the grocery store who had his own car, and I was able to secure one more usher job out of my Municipal Auditorium connection. Things were coming together well for a monumental time.

We showed up thirty minutes before the doors opened, dressed as requested in white, collared shirts and ties. Assuming there were maybe twenty ushers present, that meant that only twenty people out of the 10,000 in attendance were wearing white, short-sleeved, collared shirts and ties — we stood out like a clutch of nerds at the ultimate cool-kids convention. No bother to me, as I was there for free, while the rest of the crowd all had to stand in line for days to get tickets and drop big money to be there. The opening act for the Stones was Stevie Wonder, who was just coming into his own as a hipster, having left the "Little Stevie Wonder" of Motown behind and headed into his more artistic, groundbreaking phase of *Talking Book*, *Innervisions*, and *Songs in the Key of Life*. He could have pulled a pretty serious crowd of his own into Municipal Auditorium as the headliner, but there he was, opening for the Rolling Stones. My friend and I were seating people in the upper reaches of the auditorium, and didn't have the time or attention to enjoy Mr. Wonder. Climbing up and down the steep slopes of stairs at that arena — hastily designed and built during the WPA-funded, post-depression 1930s, prior to strict building codes that wouldn't allow for such short steps and steep angles — winded us and any who were just trying to get seated for the main attraction.

Stevie played his forty-minute set to the polite but anxious crowd, the lights went back on, and we found ourselves all dressed up, ready to party, but with no place to sit. Our thought was that if we had no seats, and we'd have to stand somewhere, we may as well head to the main floor, closer to the stage and the music. As we walked toward the doors of the main arena floor, in our white shirts and badly tied red ties, two very official-looking large men, clad in skintight ROLLING STONES T-shirts, walked up to my friend and I. They were massive, muscular as hell and mean looking; certainly they'd earned money somewhere along the line either playing professional football, or throwing skinny punks clean through the air, out of bars, casinos, or nightclubs. These guys were obviously hired security guns, professionals, and my first thought was that they were going to beat the crap out of us for wearing ties to the Rolling Stones concert.

"Are you ushers?" one of the monsters asked.

"Uh, yes, yes we are!" I squeaked.

"Where are you stationed?"

"Uh, we're not stationed anywhere right now." I figured the jig was up and we were going to make this guy's day, as I supposed he and his massive cohort had a side bet on how far they could fling a 110-pound gate-crasher.

"Follow me ..." he said, and follow him we did, through the door that opened onto the main floor of the arena and up the center aisle, walking closer with every step to the front of the stage.

I couldn't believe what was happening, as my buddy and I were too awestruck to act anything but awestruck, trying to look as if we knew what we were doing and where we were going.

The first row of seats was probably ten feet from the foot of the stage, and in between those seats and the stage was a no-man's-land, which was patrolled by six or eight other ex-football players, guys that no normal human would ever consider challenging for territorial rights, not even to get a few feet closer to Mick Jagger. And there amongst those professional giants, those hired bouncers, in that sacred no-man's-land, stood my pimply-faced, long-haired, white-shirt-and-tie-wearing skinny ass, my back literally against the foot of the stage, working crowd control for the greatest rock & roll band in the world. This all happened in a matter of minutes, faster than I could comprehend what was happening. And in a flash, the lights went off, the crowd went crazy, and Mick Jagger all but kicked me in the back of the head as he jumped onto center stage and began belting out "Brown Sugar." By absolutely no good design of my own, I was lucky enough to have the best seat in the house, at the greatest concert that was happening on earth on the night of June 22nd, 1972, and it didn't cost me a penny.

You'd think things couldn't get any better, but the night, and my string of good luck, was not yet over for the evening.

Very quickly, possibly before getting to the bridge in "Brown Sugar," I transformed from an intimidating security guard into your average concertgoer and Stones fan, albeit with way better than average seats. I could tell instantly that I was of absolutely no use to the behemoths the Stones hired to keep the crowd back, so I turned around, faced the stage, and thoroughly enjoyed the rest of the concert. Not a word of rebuke was heard from the guard that recruited me. The show flew by in a flash — fifteen fabulous songs, the band in their prime, and the atmosphere charged with an electricity that the patrons knew would only flow at this voltage but once in their lives, twice if they're lucky.

The lights came on; the Stones had left the building; and my buddy and I reunited with our ride, who had not been able to share in the largesse of Lady Luck, having stayed in the upper rafters of Municipal Auditorium, watching the show from a step in one of the aisles. It was maybe 10:00 p.m., and while I was more than ready to head home, Usher #3 had other plans to continue the Stones celebration just a little while longer.

I don't remember his name, nor could I today pick him out of a lineup of two, but I remember he was a year older than us, heading into his senior year of high school at Shawnee Mission East High School. He had a warm six-pack of Pabst Blue Ribbon in his car, which was good for two cans each; back then, that was about all I needed to enjoy myself. We cruised south, back out to the suburbs, back to the OP, and ended up on a deserted country road, which I'm now guessing was probably 135th Street, between Antioch Road and Quivira Road. It was way the hell farther out than I'd ever been, or ever had any need to be. The road was then a two-lane gravel and dirt road, totally unlit and devoid of any humanity. This was fenced-off pasture land, most likely owned by inhabitants of one of the farmhouses that slumbered peacefully in the late-night darkness. My new Shawnee Mission East friend whom I had just met that evening pulled over, turned the car off, and OMG, asked if we would like to "get high." I knew that meant smoking marijuana, and on June 22nd, 1972, at the tender age of sixteen years, I had never in my life been anywhere near marijuana. Of course, I knew all about pot, and knew it was becoming somewhat common, but absolutely not in my immediate world. I was still getting the "reefer madness" speech from my parents and elders: i.e., one puff and you'll go off the deep end and end up spending the rest of your life in a straitjacket, chained to the wall of an asylum. Whether I believed it or not, I wasn't willing to risk spending the rest of my days as a resident of the Osawatomie State Hospital.

I was in the back seat of the car, and I quietly declined the offer to get high, but my friend from Rockhurst was game. The dome light of the car was turned on, and the pothead pulled out a small pipe and began loading it with pot, or weed, as it is now more commonly called. He then struck a match, lit the bowl, and immediately the mixture began popping like hot corn in a kettle (seeds!), and the car became choked with a toxic smoke that did indeed smell like some of the local fields that I used to set on fire for kicks. (While what I am describing is so obvious and passé to many of us now, remember, I was witnessing this ceremonial ritual for the very first time.)

The smoker choked and coughed and gasped, exhaling a billowing plume of more smoke, the dimly lit car so thick with pot exhaust that I couldn't avoid ingesting a heavy dose of the stuff myself. The pipe then went to my adventurous Rockhurst cohort, and the popping, puffing, choking, and hacking was repeated. It didn't seem to be a very entertaining way to spend your idle time — it was as if they were engaged in a competition to see who could withstand the highest degree of agony.

My pulse was racing, my heart pounding, and I was terrified of the situation in which I'd gotten myself. And then the worse thing imaginable happened: I saw headlights from another car heading for us in the rearview mirror. We were not to be alone at this late hour, in the absolute middle of nowhere. My comrades also quickly noticed the car lights, and off went the dome light, and down went the windows. We remained silent and still (except for my heart, which was pounding so loudly it felt like it was shaking the car with each beat), and watched helplessly as the lights slowly got closer. Our visitor wasn't flying down the road, but cruising, ever so deliberately. As the car got close enough for us to see it, lo and behold, the first distinguishing feature was a pair of siren lights on its roof. It was one of the OP's finest, a policeman, who, unbeknownst to him, had just stumbled on a bona fide opportunity to gain his captain's stripes by having a minor marijuana cartel handed to him on a silver platter.

So here I was on an isolated country road late at night. There was no place to run, nowhere to hide, and the situation was obvious to the police officer — a beat-up car; three longish-haired young occupants; a trail of smoke wafting out of the window into the humid, dead summer air; empty beer cans on the floor; two underage drinkers in the car; and, with minimal snooping on the soon-to-be-promoted officer's part, a smoking hot pot pipe and an illegal baggie of the seediest weed this side of the nearest ditch.

As good as my luck had been to that point in the evening, it now had taken a ninety-degree downward turn. What were the odds that I'd find myself parked in the middle of nowhere, sitting in the back seat of some drug lord's car, and the one person in a million who's driving down that isolated road to nowhere at that time of night is a cop! Could my luck possibly get any worse?

I thought first of what my parents would think, and ultimately do, about this wrongdoing in which I was now engaged by association. Reform school possibly, after I got out of prison? What would the rest of my family think, my dear grandparents, my aunts and uncles? And the honest to God truth was that I didn't even partake in the unlawful activities, I was only along for the ride; hell, I didn't even know this ne'er-do-well who had driven us into an untimely date with John Law.

Then the legal logistics slammed me in the face; I was more than likely going to have to spend at least one night in the Johnson County Jail. I'd been to the Johnson County Jail when I was in the eighth grade, on a Boy Scout troop field trip, and it had such an effect on me that I had actual night terrors for a few nights after the visit. And now I was headed to that hellhole, and not with a pack of Boy Scouts! Indeed, my good luck had run out.

And then the unthinkable happened. The cop didn't stop. He didn't slow down; he didn't flash his spotlight on us; he didn't stop and call in our license plate; he didn't even turn his head in our direction. He drove right by us without even acknowledging that we existed; he just looked straight ahead and kept on cruising down that lonely, dark country road, as if he were in another world, on the way to someplace more important.

While luck in this case was not the residue of good design, it was the residue of something, and that something might have had to do with it being near the end of the officer's shift. Drug lords and cartels? Not in the OP, certainly not then. He knew we were locals, as he would have seen the Johnson county plates. Whatever we may have been doing — and he probably had a good idea — we weren't bothering anybody, and it wasn't worth him extending his evening while damn sure ruining ours. After all, this was the OP.

So, to whomever that kind police officer was who decided not to be the one to negatively alter a couple of relatively good kids' futures, I send out a heartfelt "Thank you" to wherever you may now be. I hope you've had a good, safe run of it. If you were lucky enough to spend your career being a police officer in the OP, that was more than likely the case.

What did I learn from this? I learned never to smoke pot with strangers who may not have the financial wherewithal to afford pot without seeds, and never to smoke pot in a place where you would ever be stumbled upon by the police. And I learned that I'd much rather be lucky than good!

Growing Up Catholic
IN THE OP – PART II

Rockhurst High School, affectionately known by its' attendees as "The Rock," is not in the OP. It sits majestically back from State Line Road, which is the dividing street in the Kansas City metropolitan area between Kansas and Missouri, at the 9300 block in southern Kansas City. One good thing at that time about attending Rockhurst was that it sort of brought me out of my sheltered life in the OP. While many of my Curé of Ars classmates went to Rockhurst, there were also kids from all over the city and slightly beyond — rich kids from Mission Hills; richer kids from Visitation Parish near the Country Club Plaza; not-so-rich kids from Guardian Angels, Our Lady of Good Counsel, and Redemptorist parish in midtown KC; Slavic kids from Strawberry Hill in Kansas City, Kansas; blue-collar-family kids from Raytown, Grandview, and Independence; and a few inner-city kids and a few kids from the country. I learned in pretty short order that there was more to the world than OP-suburb workhouses and a shopping mall, and what constituted "diversity" back then was indeed a worthwhile aspect of my Rockhurst education.

In my day, there were two all-male, Catholic high schools in Kansas City: Rockhurst, the Jesuit institution of higher learning located on the outer edges of the post-WWII suburban sprawl; and De La Salle, the inner-city school run by the Christian Brothers. Rockhurst High, which was established in 1910, had also previously been located in the inner-city, as an adjunct to Rockhurst College — a Jesuit institution on a smaller scale of the Marquettes and Loyolas of the world — but in 1962 was moved south of the city to meet the demands of that burgeoning baby-boomer population. After the primary Roman Catholic schoolkid goal of the attainment of sainthood, the secondary goal for most parochially educated Kansas City Catholic boys was to score well enough on the entrance exam to gain admittance to The Rock. It was certainly the primary goal for me, after having already screwed the pooch at my shot at sainthood.

My eventual attendance at Rockhurst was preceded by that of my older brother, three older cousins, and numerous other brothers of my grade-school buddies, so I'd heard plenty of horror stories about the new brand of discipline that lie ahead of me. But I didn't sweat it too much, as after eight years of witnessing, as well as personally experiencing, the sadistic proclivities of the Sisters of St. Joseph, I would be prepared for the violent antics — violence in the name of God and discipline — of the members of the Society of Jesus, otherwise known as the Jesuits. Not unlike the chasmous leap between grade-school math and high-school calculus, the ramp up of the torturous punishment that was inflicted upon us in high school by those Jesuits quickly made me pine for the pointer poking and shoulder-pressure-point-pinching methods of the nuns.

Members of recent generations — Gen Xers and Millennials in particular — will most likely read my descriptions of school discipline with mouths agape, as corporal punishment was banished from both public and private education with the advent of tort law and the excess of attorneys that followed. We can argue about the good and bad of corporal punishment until we're blue in the face. From my perspective, corporal punishment at Rockhurst wasn't much different from spending time in prison: if you played the game by the rules, you never had to worry about corporal or penal punishment. When a guy got the snot knocked out of him by a Jesuit, or in later years ended up in prison, you pretty much assumed by his daily bad demeanor that the bad ending to his story was self-written early on.

In 2017, there was a large front-page feature story in the *Kansas City Star* from an alumnus of Rockhurst who was demanding that Rockhurst, and the Society of Jesus, publicly apologize for their engagement in corporal punishment as a primary means of discipline. The student in question was a few years older than I, and I never knew him; he didn't end up graduating from Rockhurst, transferring to a nearby public high school in his junior year. When I read the article, which detailed a few of the punishments to which he was subjected, I cringed a little but shrugged my shoulders and said to myself, "Yeah, that's pretty much what happened to you if you were a f-up." My email group of classmates from the mighty Class of '74 echoed the same sentiments, to a man! You knew the rules going into Rockhurst: step out of line and it would be your ass. Your parents knew the rules going into Rockhurst, and that is one of the solid-gold reasons why they sacrificed and spent big money sending us to a school that would give us not only an excellent academic education, but also a spiritual education, and a thump on our noggin when we had one coming.

While I wasn't able to attain my first goal of sainthood, I was able to attain my second goal of matriculating in the hallowed halls of Rockhurst High School — A College Preparatory Academy. And as luck would have it, right out of the gate, my very first class on my very first day at Rockhurst was gym class with a local Kansas City living legend; talk about your baptism by fire. His name was Al Davis, known behind his back, out of respect and not derision, as "Big Al" — even kids from the public schools knew of Big Al and would tremble at the mere mention of his name. Al Davis was also the head football coach at Rockhurst, and his success on the football field was on a par with his citywide reputation as a badass. As was the case with most high school football coaches, they were classroom teachers as well, and Mr. Davis was no exception. He was a gym teacher, and he put as much fervor into teaching gym as he did into winning Missouri state football championships.

Mr. Davis was old-school tough, even by standards of the 1940s, graduating from high school in Abilene, Kansas, to serve as an eighteen-year-old combat medic on the front lines of the European theater in World War II. A few inches shy of six feet, Coach Davis was put together like an atomic fireplug: taut and stout, and ready to explode at a moment's notice. He was also cat quick for a person assembled in such a compact, dynamic package. He played quarterback for the US Army all-star team in Europe immediately after the war, and was good enough to earn a contract offer to play pro football. But football didn't pay much back then, and he had a wife and two kids to feed, so he took the sure paycheck and began teaching at Rockhurst in 1952. He would spend the next thirty-eight years of his life molding the character and earning the respect of more than eight thousand Rockhurst males. One of his dictums should be carved in stone for all the world to see and practice: "Young men need role models, not critics. Live your life the right way each day. Lead by example." Were it so, the world would be a markedly better place.

What sort of a perverse poke at me by someone that my first class at Rockhurst would be gym — not English, not History, not stuff that I enjoyed and at which I was proficient. Nope; gym class. Gym class was intimidating for me on a couple of levels, as not only would it be my first class at Rockhurst, it would be my first-ever gym class. We didn't have gym class, or even a gymnasium, at my grade school. And the only thing that I knew about gym class, and the main thing that I dreaded about gym class — beyond the drill sergeant for a teacher that I was about to experience — was the getting-naked-in-front-of-other-guys thing. I'd done it a few times in the locker room at the swimming pool and, quite frankly, I found it to be very unnerving. I didn't like looking at other packages, and I damn sure didn't want anybody looking at mine. There is no uglier spectacle than the sight of a pasty white, pot-bellied, shrunken-peckered old man strutting his stuff around a room naked; just ask my wife. But on that particular late-August morning in 1970, I had to instantly shed both my inhibitions and my tighty-whities, slip into the heretofore never worn jock strap, and march my skinny little ass onto the gym floor in my brand new blue Rockhurst Hawklet gym shorts and T-shirt.

I was one of the first ones out of the locker room, and there stood Mr. Davis, who greeted me and pointed for me to line up against the bleachers. This went on for the next few minutes as approximately two-thirds of the class was now in the gym and lined up against the bleachers. As the remaining third of the class sauntered out of the locker room, Mr. Davis had these students line up in the middle of the gym, roughly at the center of the basketball court. Finally when all were out and lined up in their respective places — all of us curious as to the game or activity that we were about to undertake — Coach Davis quickly went into his office and just as quickly returned, holding a wooden paddle the shape of, and slightly larger than, a cricket bat.

"Good morning, gentlemen!" boomed Big Al. "By God, you are about to learn lesson number one here at Rockhurst; that being, you had better move your asses when you come to this class, or I will make you wish you didn't have an ass to move." (Yes, this was a Catholic school, and yes, Coach Davis could occasionally cuss like a sailor with a nasty hangover.)

"Alright son, you're first. Grab your ankles," Mr. Davis instructed the first tardy student in the line at mid-court. (We didn't know this at the time, but this student would turn out to be one of the smuggest of wiseass, know-it-alls in our class, and we would reflect back with glee on what was about to occur for the rest of our days.)

When instructed to grab his ankles for the purpose of bending over and exposing his ass to the business end of Big Al's paddle, this Einstein thought he was being asked to participate in some sort of exercise, and he began jumping and grabbing for his ankles in midair. He did this three or four times, missing midair connections with his ankles on all occasions. Really? What did he think he would do, other than fall face first to the floor, if he had actually grabbed and held his ankles while in midair? Float maybe?

Mr. Davis stood and watched, obviously dumbfounded by what was playing out before him. Finally, he could watch no more. "By God, I've been teaching gym class for twenty years, and *never* have I had to show somebody how to grab their ankles. Keep your damn feet on the floor and bend over and grab your damn ankles!" Our gym teacher appeared to be perturbed.

With the student's butt now pointing skyward, Coach Davis reared back with the paddle and landed it so squarely on the genius's ass that he sent the student head over heels to the floor of the gym — the force of his swing impressive, his follow-through impeccable. *Ouch*, but that had to hurt.

The rest of the students in the line quickly bent over and grabbed their ankles without having to be instructed, and the resultant swats were notably less severe than that first poke of the morning, a poke so mighty that it caused Coach Davis to break a sweat.

One might think this would be the end of the brutality in our first gym class, but Big Al was just getting warmed up. No sooner had Mr. Davis instructed all of the assembled to have a seat on the floor in the center of the gym, for the purpose of hearing a speech on the other dos and don'ts of gym class, Rockhurst, and the Catholic life in general, one last straggler came casually strolling out of the locker room. He was a big goofy-looking kid, with hangdog eyes that appeared as if they were too tired to even cry, heavy-set and slump-shouldered with curly long hair, and he was not attired in the requisite Rockhurst High gym uniform. He was the antithesis of every feature that Mr. Davis looked for in a clean-cut, righteous Catholic athlete. Big Al looked at this dead man walking as if he were in fact watching a dead man walk. After a few seconds of Big Al, with his jaw dropped nearly to his waist, staring at this sauntering idiot, the coach all but exploded. "BY GOD, WHAT IN THE HELL DO **YOU** THINK **YOU'RE** DOING?"

It is important to note that the actual date of this exchange preceded the movie *Taxi Driver*, and I swear that this is how our dawdler responded, as casually as if he were conversing with a blank wall: "Are you talkin' to me?"

Like a hungry puma with a helpless fawn in its sights, Coach Davis lunged and flew through the air at this doofus, his arms outstretched as he viciously grabbed the kid by the shoulders and pushed him with such force into the retracted bleachers that the lad left his feet and landed in a pile at Coach Davis's feet. (This kid was big, and the sight of Coach Davis throwing him against the bleachers like a rag doll was profoundly impressive, and it sent a universally received message to all who witnessed the act.)

Mr. Davis then began kicking the kid, who was now tightly curled up into a fetal position, with all of the fervor and zeal that one might use if they were getting paid by the kick. After about a thousand dollars worth of kicks, Coach Davis reached down and grabbed the student by one of his arms and dragged him across the gym floor into the locker room, out of sight but not out of earshot, as the cacophonous beating and banging of the body being repeatedly thrown against the metal lockers, and the muffled epitaphs that Big Al was continually spewing, found its way through the walls to the assembled students, our knees knocking in terrified unison.

This all happened within the first fifteen minutes of my higher education. My God, what on Earth had I done, intentionally putting myself in harm's way in such a fashion? For certain that morning I learned that "Are you talkin' to me?" was not an acceptable answer to a question posed by our gym teacher, nor probably any of the other educators at The Rock.

A slightly more genteel method of discipline practiced at Rockhurst was the demerit card; every student was given a new one quarterly and required to carry it at all times. There were twenty numbers on the card, and if you screwed up in any form or fashion — forgetting to bring a book to class, showing up late for class, goofing off in the halls between classes; i.e., minor infractions that didn't earn the time and physical effort of a full-bore ass-kicking — the teacher would initial either one or two of the numbers, and you'd have yourself one or two demerits. When you reached five demerits, the teacher would take the card and turn it in to the Dean of Students, who would eventually summon you to his office. Getting five demerits was referred to as getting JUG, which stood for "Justice Under God." JUG meant that you either had to do some sort of penance that usually involved free labor for the school, like cleaning up after a football game, or setting up for an event, or, you could opt for "swats" from the Dean of Students. During my tenure at Rockhurst, the Dean of Students was a gentleman named Ron Windmueller; he was not a priest, but kind of a priest-in-training, or in Society of Jesus parlance, a "Brother." Brother Windmueller was extremely well-liked by all of the students, as he was a big, jolly, balding guys' guy of a guy, well-suited in his position of fairly disciplining, wisely counseling, and fatherly mentoring 800 Catholic adolescent males.

In my four years at Rockhurst, I received JUG twice — the first week I was at Rockhurst, and the last week of my senior year. Both times I opted for the slave labor as penance, preferring not to have someone the size of Brother Windmueller playing baseball with my butt as the ball. I'd heard about getting five swats (one for each demerit) from Brother Windmueller, who would use his old fraternity paddle. The story was: you only felt the first one, as the pain was so intense it essentially deadened the feeling in your cheeks to the extent that you couldn't feel the final four swats, at least not until the next day, at which point you could barely walk, and not sit at all. My only guess as to why he bothered to deliver those last four blows was simply for exercise; as I mentioned, Brother Windmueller, while certainly not out of shape, was a tad on the portly side. The main reason behind the administration of these five blows of death wasn't based upon any prurient or sadistic tendencies inherent in Brother Windmueller. Rather, Brother Ron first and foremost wanted you to be responsible, be timely, and behave. Not unlike Coach Davis's opening day salvo, if you suffered at the hands of the Jesuits, you certainly earned it, and God save both your body and your soul if you crossed the line to earn it on multiple occasions. Those five swats and that locker room beatdown had a pretty effective way of getting their points across.

While the motives behind Brother Ron's swats were pure, I know for certain that I witnessed several incidents of pain inducement that I believe were less than such and were born from some sort of sado-sexual tendencies that a few of these Jesuits carried with them in the deep, dark recesses of their psyches.

I witnessed a teacher sit on the edge of a student's desk, one hand grabbing a healthy lock of the student's hair for the purpose of holding the student's head steady, with the other hand softly slapping each cheek — left then right then left then right — all the while continuing to wax eloquent on the merits of the sonnets of Gerard Manley Hopkins, never missing a beat. During this, the teacher was actually looking skyward, in a dreamlike way, as if just thinking about the ABBA-ABBA-CD-CD-CD rhyme scheme of the sonnets of which he was speaking had transposed him into another dimension, and he was totally unaware of the fact that he was causing this poor student's cheeks to turn the color of strawberry Fanta. Needless to say, the last thing that the class was paying attention to was the purity of a sonnet's rhyme scheme, as all watched in horrified fascination as the trance-induced teacher kept slapping away, gently but repeatedly. If memory serves me, that young student opted out of Rockhurst at the end of his freshman year.

Another celebrated member of the Rockhurst Corporal Punishment Hall of Fame was a gentleman named Mr. Edward Acker. He was an English teacher, and a damned good one — famed amongst the Rockhurst English department for being a master of teaching the Xs and Os of the English language — a sixty-year-old, white-haired ex-Jesuit with the build of a bowling ball set upon two tree trunks. He was short and squat and round, and walked about the room at a pace that gave one the impression he'd invented slow motion. Mr. Acker was also a heavy smoker, sucking down a nonfiltered Camel in two or three long drags, seemingly never even exhaling. He did this during class, while he was teaching. His voice was a quiet, deep, all-but-unintelligible croak, and the cadence of his speech was as slow as his method of locomotion.

It was midmorning, the third class of my first day at Rockhurst, and Mr. Acker was at the blackboard with his back to the class, cigarette in one hand, chalk in the other, staring at the board in search of his next thought, when one of my insane, uninformed classmates put the palm of his hand to his mouth and cheek and exhaled, making a faux fart sound that broke the silence in the room, drawing but a few muffled snickers.

Mr. Acker's massive head, with its long curly white hair and glasses so thick that his eyes were magnified, looking like deep blue pools, turned slowly around, not unlike an owl's head, to search for the perpetrator of this childish outburst. He noticed that all of the students were straight-faced, except for the guilty party who was wearing a shit-eating grin, more out of nervousness than bravado.

Without saying a word, Mr. Acker slowly put the chalk in the tray, turned, and picked up an ashtray from his desk. This ashtray was quite special: a round, four-inch diameter emerald-blue glass object with four two-inch round feet holding it above the surface of the desk; it weighed about six pounds. Ashtray in one hand and cigarette in the other, Mr. Acker began a snaillike procession towards the back of the classroom, his eyes fixed hard on one student, the now-former wearer of a shit-eating grin. As he trudged towards the student, the cigarette went slowly up to his mouth, the loud sound of his sucking being all but drowned out by the louder sound of the fire raging within that tobacco-laden inferno, the smoke forever disappearing into the netherworlds of Mr. Acker's respiratory system. While the walk towards the back of the room was no more than twenty feet from Mr. Acker's desk, it seemed an eternity to all assembled. It was actually a long enough stroll for the funny farter to begin developing beads of sweat, as he had no idea what would happen to him if and when Mr. Acker eventually reached his destination.

Finally, Mr. Acker stood astride the desk of the student, and in his heavy-smokers' basso profundo, audible only to the perp and the few students immediately next to him, he asked, "Are you responsible for the noise ...?"

Once again, a wet-behind-the-ears Rockhurst freshman made the mistake of answering a question from a Rockhurst educator with a question. "What noise are you talking about ... Mister Acker?"

The next move from Mr. Acker belied his normally painstakingly slow mode of locomotion, as his right hand, the one holding the mega ashtray, raised quickly and came crashing down on the crown of the student's thick skull before the kid could even flinch. But flinch he certainly did. The sound made when the ashtray rapped on his noggin was literally that of a hammer on a coconut, both wooden and hollow. The force of such a blow would have knocked most people cold, but not this crazy/brave tough-guy comedian. His face scrunched up in agony, but he held steady, his eyes coming to a cross-eyed glaze as the initial sting of the blow started to cool.

Mr. Acker stood and stared at his victim, watching as the shit-eating grin reappeared on the student's face, this time not intentionally, but as a result of his innate stupidity kicking in from the force of the blow.

Mr. Acker then croaked, "Don't ever again do that in my classroom ..." and slowly turned away from the starstruck student and began the slow parade march back to the front of the room, where he placed the ashtray on his desk, took one last, protracted drag off his cigarette, snubbed it into the ashtray, and then casually picked up the chalk and began writing examples of gerunds and infinitives on the blackboard.

The most violent act, and the act with the most potential to inflict serious bodily harm to its recipient, involved the triplet combination of the last teacher I would have expected to inflict harm, a metal ruler, and the biggest wiseass in our class.

Our freshman year we were grouped in classes of thirty students according to the scores on our entrance exams, so at least by that measuring stick, we would all be in the same ballpark with regards to our mental acuity. You would have the same classes all day with the same thirty students, so you got to know the guys in your group pretty well. On this particular day, our wiseass brings to school a metal ruler; it was a big ruler, maybe three inches in width and a solid quarter-of-an-inch thick. The most important feature of this ruler, and the feature most germane to this story, was the amount of noise it made when dropped on the tiled classroom floor.

CLANGCLANGCLANGCLANGCLANGclang-clangclangclangclangclangclangclang…

The ruler-dropping game started in French class, right out of the gate in our second class of the day. Midway through the class, the ruler hits the floor, and the din of the clanging echoes throughout the room, bringing the teacher to an abrupt stop. The entire class instantly turns to the back of the room to see who in the hell would risk their life by doing something so foolish, and there sat the perpetrator with a Cheshire-cat grin on his face that was possibly wider than the twelve-inch piece of steel that he'd just jettisoned from the surface of his desk. The French teacher had a bit of a reputation as a softie, and his only admonition was "Mr. Webber, make certain that doesn't happen again."

The third hour of the day was typing class, and even amongst the din of thirty Smith Corona manual typewriters, the CLANG of the landing ruler overrode the CLACK of the collective thirty keys per second that were being struck against the thirty sheets of typing paper. This time our perpetrator dropped the ruler twice, as the first drop went unnoticed by the typing teacher, but not by the student's twenty-nine other classmates, who were quick to see a pattern developing for what we'd all initially assumed would be another quiet, studious day at The Rock.

The next couple of classes went the same, with a few small exceptions: in Biology, the teacher casually walked back to the student and confiscated the ruler until the end of class; and in History, the teacher calmly walked back to the student, confiscated the ruler, smacked the student once HARD across the back of his neck (*WHAP!* vs. CLANG), and walked back to the front of the class to resume his teaching. In another act of minor insanity, the teacher returned the ruler to the student at the end of class.

We'd made it to eighth period with but a few bumps and bruises, no spilled blood, and a wiseass with a welt on the back of his neck and an irritating ruler still in his possession. Up the stairs we trudged to the third floor and made a quick right turn into our last class of the day. Rockhurst had three floors with three main sets of stairs equally distributed along the length of the rectangular structure. The stairwells were ten feet wide, with eight stairs up to a landing, then eight more stairs up to the floor. (Why this detail? Just hang in there with me.)

Our final class of the day was Freshman Algebra, taught by Mr. Lowe, a lay teacher who was about as laid back as a guy could be. You didn't do your homework? He didn't care, nor would he give you a demerit; he'd just give you an F. You didn't pay attention in class? He didn't care; he'd just give you an F when you failed the test. After all, it was his opinion that your parents were paying big money to send you to this fancy-schmancy school, and if you didn't want to learn, you could deal with the consequences that you'd suffer at home.

Mr. Lowe was also a bit of a beatnik, as he was a child of the pre-60s hippie generation; i.e., those that planted the seeds that sprouted peace, love, and understanding. Mr. Lowe was also the first person that I recall preaching the gospel of volunteerism, the inequality inherent in our system, and social justice. Simply put, when compared to most of the other ballbusters at Rockhurst High, Mr. Lowe seemed like a pretty cool guy, and way ahead of any curve that I'd yet to encounter. Little would I have imagined that this contemporary of the Beat Generation, this proponent of social justice, would perpetrate the most aggressive act of classroom justice that I would ever see in my twelve years of private, parochial education.

About halfway through the algebra class, almost on cue, the ruler hit the classroom floor with all the gusto of the previous ten drops. Mr. Lowe glanced over his shoulder from the blackboard in the direction of the clatter and din, but didn't miss a beat as he continued scribbling what appeared to me to be a mixture of hieroglyphics and ancient colloquial Chinese. Possibly as little as five minutes later, the ruler danced upon the floor for what would be its absolute final fling. Mr. Lowe quietly put down his chalk and began walking to the back of the classroom, and not unlike a few of his peripatetic pedagogues earlier in the day, continued teaching, seemingly unnerved by the loud disruption of the errant ruler. As he neared the desk of Webber the Wiseass, he broke stride linguistically and said, "Needless to say, this is going to be the last time we'll have this interruption today."

Mr. Lowe bent over, picked the ruler up from the floor, and began walking up the aisle back to the front of the classroom. Halfway up the aisle, he quickly whirled around 180° to further address the wiseass, and what did he see but Mr. Ruler-Dropping Dead Man flipping him the biggest bird of all birds; a more defiant gesture I have never witnessed. If giving someone the finger could be categorized as an aggressive, near violent act, this particular finger-giving was all but lethal in its deliverance. If you could attach a volume switch to giving someone the bird, this bird would have shouted down a tornado.

The room became so quiet you could have heard a fly fart. Mr. Lowe stood still for about ten seconds, and I believe that I noticed him begin to tremble, his right eye twitching a bit and his upper lip breaking into the slightest hint of a quiver. As Mr. Lowe carefully pondered his next move, the defiant bird that had stabbed into the air like Lady Liberty's torch slowly receded, and the wiseass clutched both sides of his desktop, grasping for something solid, readying himself for the inevitable onslaught. There was no Cheshire-cat grin this time from Mr. Webber. Rather, he had the nervous smile one might exhibit upon discovering that a flatulation was in fact more solid than gas.

Then, as quick as the snap of a finger, Mr. Lowe covered the ten feet between he and the wiseass in two long steps and grabbed the corners of the desktop adjacent to young Webber's hands. (These were the old one-piece desks with the seat and the desktop attached.) He began pulling the desk up the aisle at a rapid rate of speed, while all others in the aisle quickly pushed their desks to the side to get out of harm's way, as it was obvious that the infliction of collateral damage was the last concern on Mr. Lowe's mind.

As he pulled, he huffed and puffed, out of breath from anger and not the physical act in which he was currently engaged, "You … will … take … your … sorry … ass … down … to … Brother's office … and … tell him … exactly … what … you've … done, and … I'll be down … when I'm finished teaching … students … that give a shit!"

In fact, the last half of this tirade was barely audible, as Mr. Lowe had dragged the desk, with Webber still seated in it, out of the room and a short way down the hall. We then heard banging and clanging that made a day's worth of Webber's ruler dropping pale in comparison as Mr. Lowe heaved the desk down the flight of eight stairs to the landing between the second and third floors.

Mr. Lowe came back into the room noticeably out of breath from the exertion of hammer-throwing the student and his desk down the stairs. He gathered himself for a few seconds, calmly and carefully smoothed his hair back, and said, "Now, where was I? Oh yes, here's that neat little trick involving integers that I was about to show you ..."

To this day it is not known if Webber actually made the ride down those stairs still in the desk, or if he leapt from the airborne furniture in the nick of time, much as an occupant of a runaway car would eject before flying over a cliff. What is known for certain is that we never saw Webber again at Rockhurst. What we are unsure of is: did he get expelled, did he quit, or was he dead and buried from injuries suffered in his headlong, down-the-stairs pas de deux with his desk?

No question, I was both excited and terrified as to what the second semester of my freshman year would bring, as well as the ensuing three years beyond. If I learned one thing that first semester at Rockhurst, it was what not to do if I intended to get through my high school years in one piece. Justice Under God indeed!

One might wonder — especially younger readers who were raised in a corporal-punishment-free educational environment — why on earth students would willingly subject themselves to the rigidities of a Rockhurst. That is an even crazier question when you consider that the local public high schools that serviced the OP, namely the Shawnee Mission Unified School District, were exceptional schools, amongst the best in the nation. Oh — and they were tuition free!

First and foremost, there was the spiritual development that came with a Rockhurst education. That wasn't pounded into you as much as it was in elementary Catholic school, but it was there for you to whatever degree you wanted to avail yourself. Most of us did.

With a Rockhurst education came the tradition and history that was shared by generations of Rockhurst families and friends. With Rockhurst High School being founded in 1921, many of my classmate's fathers, and even some grandfathers, attended Rockhurst. As I mentioned earlier, it was drilled into you at an early age that when you came of age, you went to Rockhurst.

There weren't any females attending Rockhurst, which was bad on many levels, but okay on others; without females, you tended to keep your eye on the educational ball a bit more, as there wasn't the ever-present public-school distraction of burgeoning female breasts and bottoms. Not having females around also eliminated the innate competition amongst hormone-laden males to grab the eye and curry the favor of the females — no need for any peacocks at the Rock as we were all a bunch of pimple-faced, fuzzy-chinned dorks, dressed similarly in khaki pants and collared cotton shirts.

And then there were the Jesuits, who in addition to their mastery of arcane torture techniques were also teachers extraordinaire. The Society of Jesus is a religious order of the Catholic Church, founded by a Spaniard, Ignatius of Loyola, in 1540 for the purpose of spreading the Word of God and educating the uninformed. The Jesuits are responsible for a number of very fine educational institutions in the United States, including Georgetown University, Gonzaga University, Boston College, and Marquette University, to name but a few. I'm not saying you necessarily got a better education at Rockhurst than at public schools, but I do believe that opportunity was available through a more culture-laden curriculum. I didn't go to the OP public schools, but I have many close friends who did, and using them as a barometer, I know I was exposed to things, particularly in the arts, that you didn't naturally stumble upon at Shawnee Mission Directional.

Finally, there was the camaraderie of the all-male, one-for-all-and-all-for-one environment. As the comic-book violence I've described was perpetrated equally to one and all who screwed up, it tended to bind us together in our mutual quest for self-survival. Soldiers don't typically survive combat together without ultimately being joined at the hip. To this day, a large percentage of my class of '74 stays in touch: monthly lunches and get togethers at local watering holes, all-but-daily email and text chains. Possibly the small size of our graduating class — roughly 180 students — plays into this, versus the Shawnee Mission schools, whose class sizes were fivefold that number. None of the public-school guys I know today still keep in touch with more than one or two of their closest high school friends.

Rockhurst High School still ranks as one of the best high schools in the Kansas City metropolitan area, for most of the same reasons as it was in my day. Fortunately for today's generation of thinner-skinned, more emotionally brittle high schoolers, Rockhurst is now sans a Jesuit or two who might have been prone to the occasional display of sadistic predispositions. Rockhurst also has the distinction of being one of two high schools in the United States with two sitting United States senators as alumni: Senator Tim Kaine of Virginia, and Senator Josh Hawley of Missouri — one liberal, the other conservative, which also speaks nicely to Rockhurst offering a well-rounded education. Put simply, Rockhurst High School was a hell of a tough place to go to, but a wonderful place to come from — never mind that I might have gotten clocked by Mr. Acker's ashtray for such a horribly constructed sentence.

Grown Up IN THE OP

It's been forty-five-plus years since I grew up in the OP and lived the stories that I've detailed in these pages. During those past four decades I went away to college in Lawrence, Kansas, came back to the OP, married and moved to Fairway, Kansas, and then Shawnee, Kansas, where I raised a family and had a career.

In 2007, my wife, Julie, and I totally bugged out of both the area and reality, selling our house and moving to the mountains of Colorado after purchasing a historic, century-old hotel, bar, and restaurant named the Riverside Hotel on the banks of the Colorado River, in the little town of Hot Sulphur Springs, Colorado. Our adventures at the Riverside Hotel are chronicled in my first book, *Living Life Riverside: Our Nightmarish Pursuit of the American Dream.* Although it was only 724 road miles away from the OP, it may as well have been as far from the OP as the planet Jupiter, certainly when comparing how we spent the first twenty years of our life together working and raising our family in a Midwestern postcard of normalcy. Other than now having the occasional stranger buy me a drink in a bar in exchange for hearing some of the unbelievable stories from our Colorado sojourn, the experience left us broke, humbled, and failed. We fought hard for three years, but those beastly mountains won, sending us off in search of a plan to restore our lives and our livelihood.

God and good fortune rescued us with a job opportunity in Jackson, Mississippi, which we accepted graciously and without hesitation. In March of 2010, we packed what little we had left and drove 1,334 miles from the Rocky Mountains to our rental home and new life in Brandon,

Mississippi, experiencing a culture shift that more than doubled down on our OP to Colorado move. Mississippi can be as charming as any place in the country; the weather was considerably warmer than in the Rockies, and that warmth transcended itself right through the hearts of the residents, who welcomed us with open arms. However, it was pointed out to us on endless occasions that we were Yankees, which meant that we'd have to find a round hole into which we could pound our square, Northern frames.

While living in Mississippi was a financial blessing, and the job and lifestyle were all but sedentary when compared to running a hotel, bar, and restaurant, there was the ever-present feeling that, as our dear fellow Kansan Dorothy Gale used to say, "There's no place like home!" Shortly into our Mississippi adventure, I started looking for opportunities that would get us back to the OP: back to our friends, our families, and, most importantly, back to the blanket of comfort under which we were raised. The true tipping point came when our closest family members started dying: my mother and sister, Julie's mother and best friend. That woke us up to the reality of just how far we'd strayed from home.

After three short/long years in Mississippi, an employment door opened that thankfully brought us back home, back to the OP. We found a beautiful house near 95th and Nall, just blocks from all three of the homes in which I grew up, and right in the midst of all my old haunts: Metcalf South, The Drumstick Restaurant, Riley's Gulf Station, the Kroger Supermarket (with a Cakebox Bakery), and the SupeRx Drugstore, to name but a few.

As we headed north, I wondered if they'd yet raised the price of a large Coke to fifty cents at The Drumstick?

But it's now 2020. The Drumstick is no more, replaced by a liquor store, which at my current stead in life is a pretty good trade-off. Riley's Gulf has become a Shell station, without Mr. Riley's top-notch car service station, and, more importantly, no more an emporium for giveaway matchbooks, nor a place to hang out on a hot summer afternoon. Kroger and SupeRx are now a Sprouts, a feel-good, healthyish, vegan-friendly store where you can only buy off-brand products that you've never heard of for twice the price that you'd pay for name brands anywhere else. But hey, they seem to be selling these expensive things for the greater good, and the hipsters who shop there don't seem to notice or complain that it's as corporate and profit-driven as Amazon or Walmart. What the hell; we've all got to make a buck, eh?

Another unsettling thing that confronted me upon my return back home to the OP was the seemingly overnight disappearance of one of the neighborhood mainstays, Meadowbrook Country Club, a place we had skirted the perimeters of on an all-but-daily basis as kids: looking, longing, and wanting nothing more than to swim in that pool, star on those tennis courts, and defile the pristine flora of that magnificent golf course with our flailing three-irons.

Meadowbrook Country Club is no longer, having been replaced not too long ago by a beautiful, extremely functional park, replete with walking trails, lakes, a playground on steroids that is even grand by the standards of millennials, and fabulous green spaces. It also contains a massive apartment complex, named The Kessler, that resembles a modern-day version of the Palace of Versailles, had King Louis XIV been working under a tight budget when building the original. It's named after Arv Kessler, a Meadowbrook member whose double eagle on the fourteenth hole of the old golf course, during the 1965 club championship, is still the stuff of legend. As one of Arv's foursome famously stated after his momentous drive, "Old Arv sure does know how to put the wood to it!"

The rest of the development has a Marriott hotel, an upscale restaurant that requires a Google food app to know what type of pretentious pasta you're ordering, uber-pricy duplexes, and multimillion-dollar homes, stacked so closely together that you could count the grains of salt your next-door neighbor shakes upon his scrambled eggs as you look out your window and watch him eat his breakfast. Under construction at the time of this writing is a Senior Living and Eldercare facility at the southwest corner of the property. My wife jokes that all the place is missing is a cemetery: from your birth in the Kessler, to your duplex and single-home upgrades during your high-earning years, right into assisted living, eldercare, and then the cemetery at the end of the game. Cradle-to-grave in one-half square mile of suburbia.

Metcalf South Shopping Center has also been obliterated from the face of the earth, with not a shred of its existence in evidence beyond the stand-alone, unoccupied structure that was the Sears anchor at the south end of the mall. The Glenwood Manor, a first-rate hotel and conference complex, is long gone, along with The Glenwood Theater, which was, at its time, *the* finest movie house in all of Kansas City. It was where I saw, on a massive wide screen, in reclining chairs, *The Godfather* and *Godfather:*

Part II, Jaws, Close Encounters of the Third Kind, Star Wars, and every other major movie from 1966 until 1999.

Speaking of movie theaters, OP kids no longer go to the Overland Theater in downtown Overland Park on a Saturday afternoon to watch the latest oater, monster, or science fiction movie. One of my great childhood memories was a Saturday afternoon spent with my older brother, Ron; and the Corrigan brothers, Greg and Brian, watching the rock and roll movie, the *T.A.M.I. Show,* which featured The Beach Boys, The Rolling Stones, but most importantly, James Brown, the unquestioned Godfather of Soul. On this particular Saturday, James Brown was just a little bit ahead of the curve for this less-than-diverse crowd of OP youngsters, we who screamed with unbridled delight at his performance, so much so that the theater owner stopped the film, came to the front of the theater, and told us that any more such outbursts would be the end of the show. Back to the movie, and back to James Brown shaking, shimmying, falling to the stage in a state of rapture, then having a shawl wrapped around his shoulders and being helped to his feet by his attendants; and back to an audience full of mesmerized OP kids howling in delight — and the movie stopped, the lights went on, and we were all told to hit the streets. The line at the pay phone for an early ride home was around the block. The theater is still there, sadly not filled with kids during a weekend matinee, but hopefully holding the ghosts of my adolescent Saturday afternoons of popcorn, Good & Plenty, and James Brown in all of his soulful glory.

Neither do you walk the neighborhoods of the OP and see fourteen-year-old kids cutting lawns or shoveling snow-filled driveways for their spending money. Landscape companies barely existed back in the day, as every able-bodied teenager competed with the next-door neighbor for the right to cut the Johnson's lawn, rake and bag the fallen leaves in the Neiman's yard, or shovel the Effbaum's driveway after an OP snowfall. Now it's one hundred different landscape companies that have displaced summer, fall, and winter employment opportunities for today's suburban fourteen-year-old. Sadly, I don't think today's kids know, or would mind, that their primary source of tax-free income has been plucked from them.

Nor do you see today's kids playing flag football in the front yard, or Wiffle Ball in the backyard, where you'd just hope for a pitch sweet enough to whack that plastic ball over the fence into the neighbor's yard, or, God forbid, you used a real baseball, and drilled that leather-clad missile through your neighbor's basement window, which I did on one occasion. The ball was hit so purely that it didn't even shatter the window but left a clean, smoking hole the precise size of a baseball in the middle of the assaulted pane of glass.

What do OP teenagers do today for fun or for commerce? Is it all video games and handheld technology for fun? With few opportunities for commerce, is their folly fully funded by their parents? Mine certainly wasn't. The malls where we all worked in the day are now closed, leaving very few stores where a kid can work, earn, and learn what's necessary to survive in this world; that won't get any better with the insurgence of online purchasing. Our beautiful Metcalf South, French Market, and Venture have been replaced by Home Depot and Lowes, and those stores are now staffed not by OP teenagers, but by OP baby boomers, who are all trying to hang on and occupy themselves after their corporate gigs have gone south — and, oh, maintain their health insurance.

There is another important change that applied not only to Overland Park, but to all other Midwestern suburban enclaves, which were predominantly inhabited by middle- and upper-middle-class whites. That is certainly not the case in the current OP, nor most any other major Midwestern suburb. Growing up in the early sixties, diversity wasn't a term that had even made it into our cultural lexicon. This wasn't good or bad, or right or wrong; this was simply how it was, and it was how our lives were formed. Our growing up in an environment that lacked diversity didn't naturally make us bigots, or racists, or evil people. We were simply naïve to the intricacies of sharing space with other colors and cultures. Gratefully, we've advanced beyond that point.

Now, living in a more diverse OP brings me back to a story regarding what was a profound lack of diversity in the early OP '60s. If you want to read about politics, race, privilege, hatred, etc., there are thousands of books and Internet articles to read, digest, and debate. This is just an innocent story that comes from the heart.

The year was 1963, and I was seven years old. I went to the Barnum & Bailey Circus at Municipal Auditorium in downtown Kansas City as a guest of a neighbor and his father. We sat up in the nosebleed seats, probably the cheapest seats, but as a kid I remember exclaiming that the seats were awesome, as up here, "We can see everything!" Sitting next to me throughout the show was a young black kid about my age. At the time I thought that he was just about one of the nicest kids I had ever met, and we talked and laughed and had one heck of a great time throughout the show, more enjoying each other's company than what was going on with the animals and acrobats in the three rings that lay far below us. As we left, we said we'd see each other again, and I truly hoped that would be the case. The next day I told my parents about the new friend I'd made at the circus, mentioning in passing that he was black, and told them we planned on getting together in the future. They challenged me on this, saying that probably wasn't going to happen because he wasn't from around here, the OP. It was at this point that I pulled a lie out of my pocket — something I would do with my parents a multitude of times over the next twenty years of my life — and told them that I had actually met this kid before, and he *did* live in the OP. "Really; where have you met him before the circus?" asked one of my parents. Quick as a fib, I answered, "I've played with him at Brookridge," the country club to which we belonged. Both parents immediately burst out laughing at what they knew was an obvious lie, as anyone, other than a child, would know that there were no black members of Brookridge, or any other suburban country club, in 1963. How sad was the fact that this fun little kid that I'd met and had a great time with couldn't swim in the same pool as me; but how wonderful was the fact that I, as a child, wouldn't have known this to be the case, or imagined it to even be an issue.

My how we've changed. Father Time is not only a poor caretaker of beauty, but he is also an outright obliterator of innocence. The last forty years have seen the transformation of a lot of the essential peripheral stuff — economic, social, political, racial, and environmental — in not only the OP but also the rest of the world. I'll get beyond the loss of innocence and the changes you encounter after time does its thing, you grow up, move away, and return to your home, your womb, because the OP is still as good a place as you can live, day-to-day, buck-to-buck, as anywhere on the planet. Sure, there's no Harrods department store in the OP, no Grand Canyon National Park, no French Laundry restaurant, and no Champs-Élysées Avenue. But there is a plethora of verdant real estate upon which you can safely subsist in excellent fashion, day-to-day, every day, as if the Grand Canyon was your backyard, The French Laundry was your kitchen, and the Champs-Élysées was your favorite stretch of Metcalf. And the keys you own may not open the front door of Harrods but at one time did unlock the sliding glass door of Thom McAn shoe store at the Metcalf South Shopping Center.

Acknowledgements

Thanks are in order to the following for their help in putting this book together.

Brad Moore and the Overland Park Historical Society for their help in assembling and supplying many of the photos, and their counsel and direction regarding facts, figures, dates and places. If you care about the OP, you might want to consider joining the Overland Park Historical Society, if not for your sake, then certainly for the sake of future generations. (www.ophistorical.org)

Dawn Petersen, who once again quietly and supportively suffered through the editing process.

Lori Bennett, of Lori Bennett Design, whose fine imagination brought the beginning, middle and end of this book to its beautiful, visual culmination.

The Sisters of Saint Joseph and Cure of Ars Grade School, The Society of Jesus and Rockhurst High School, and all that had a hand in saving me from the throes of paganism, and giving me the feedstuff for such wonderful memories.

William T. Haupt, Larry Cavener, Richard Short, Roclan Robbins and Frank Melville for their efforts in molding a high-quality lump of clay into a self-sustaining tax payer.

A special thanks to Little Timmy and his baby elephant, for providing me the time and inspiration to make this book a reality.

And finally, my sincere apologies to The OP Fire Department, Mr. Reed Austin, Mr. Phil Spitter, the numerous, innocent prank-call recipients, and to anyone upon who's car I tied a bag of urine.

www.ingramcontent.com/pod-product-compliance
Lightning Source LLC
Chambersburg PA
CBHW021953290426
44108CB00012B/1053